Danci

in the Desert

Dancing in the Desert

Prayers and reflections for Lent

Sally Foster-Fulton

wild goose
publications

www.ionabooks.com

First published 2016 by
Wild Goose Publications,
Fourth Floor, Savoy House,
140 Sauchiehall Street, Glasgow G2 3DH, UK,
the publishing division of the Iona Community.
Scottish Charity No. SC003794.
Limited Company Reg. No. SC096243.

ISBN 978-1-84952-457-5

Cover image © Velvia8 | Dreamstime.com

Overseas distribution
Australia: Willow Connection Pty Ltd, Unit 4A, 3-9 Kenneth Road,
Manly Vale, NSW 2093
New Zealand: Pleroma, Higginson Street, Otane 4170, Central Hawkes Bay
Canada: Novalis/Bayard Publishing & Distribution, 10 Lower Spadina Ave.,
Suite 400, Toronto, Ontario M5V 2Z2

Printed by Bell & Bain, Thornliebank, Glasgow

Contents

Introduction

Dancing in the Desert is a collection of reflections and prayers written to lead you into that quiet space that helps you hear yourself more clearly. Lent is a time to listen, to learn about the you that unites to everything that breathes the air or bends in the breeze. If you listen intently, you may hear the Spirit whisper, 'Shall we dance?'

If you let yourself go, you may find that your soul learns new steps and, in time, moves in time to the music usually muffled by busyness. Listen … to the beat of your heart.

Listen … to the cries and the cheers of your brothers and sisters.

Listen … to the song sung by God's created and cherished world.

Let Lent in and may the dance begin.

Thank you to my wonderful husband, Stuart, whose love has held me like an embrace, whose patience and wisdom has made my writing and work possible, and whose being mine makes it all so much more fun! This book is for you.

Sally Foster-Fulton

On baptism

Stripped-away God

Stripped-away God,
you stand exposed before us.
Cradling you naked at your birth,
we wrapped you in swaddling bands,
enfolded your arrival in angel song, star-shine
and mystery.

Now, emboldened by your baptism,
you emerge from the waters.
With the trappings torn off,
with your gifts thrown open and waiting,
with the story of the infant
seen in stark contrast to the man,
we stand by the bank and wonder:
who are you and what do you want from us?
When we see you, wet from the water, restless
and ready to walk into the wilderness,
divested of all pretense,
we are the ones who feel vulnerable.

Stripped-away God,
you stand exposed before us
and we struggle to stand with you.
Cleansed and calm, you are almost ready to begin,
but there is one thing lacking.
And then the sound pierces our sight
and we are momentarily enlightened:
'This is my son, the beloved, with whom I am well-pleased.'

Stripped away of all other claims,
this alone remains – love.
Let us follow where it leads.

Spirit descending

We don't find space enough any more; we don't find time – and that's a shame. Because sometimes we need a moment of clarity if we're going to hear what God has to say to us …

Let the Spirit of God descend now …
into the space we open in our souls.
Hear the words that are far too often drowned out
in our noisy quest for the world's idea of perfection:
'You are my beloved – with you I am well-pleased.'

Remain in that space and know you are loved.

God of us all, you called Jesus your beloved.
And because we are yours through him
we inherit that call and mantle.
Help us to live as a people in whom you can be well-pleased.

God of us all,
give us patience with each other.
We need to remember how hard it is to be human,
that we share a frailty and a beauty,
that growing and learning and becoming
is inherent in every soul.

God of us all,
pour your kindness into our spirits:
give us the empathy it takes to change for each other
because only when we begin where we are
will we ever begin to turn the world
back onto a path of peace.

When we fail, pick us up;
when we falter, give us strength;
when we feel that our feeble attempts are a waste,
show us another glimpse of eternity
and lead us to that space where our souls
can hear your words again:
'You are my beloved.'

God of us all, be near.
Amen

'I love you, boy'

What else was there to say really? After he stripped off the clothes that protected him, shed the average life that was waiting to welcome him; left them behind on the shore of the Jordan and waded vulnerable into that water, aligning himself forever with controversy.

What else could a parent say to a child at that point – when protection wasn't an option, when pride didn't begin to cover it? What else was there to say really? Nothing except: *'This is my son, the Beloved, with whom I am well-pleased.'* And so, at his baptism, we are invited to hear God whisper: 'I love you, boy' into his ear as he comes clean in the River Jordan.

The transformational power of those words 'I love you' …

When embraced, they travel with you – ground you and send you out – you will never be the same once those words sink in.

Jesus, fresh from those words 'You are my beloved', is led into the wilderness – he could never go back to who he was before; and if we join him in his baptism, neither can we.

Jesus came to the River Jordan, stripped off the clothes that protected him, shed the average life that was waiting to welcome him; left them behind on the shore of the Jordan and waded vulnerable into that water, aligning himself forever with controversy.

He will live and die for this new love he has found. He will live and die with the words he heard whispered as he emerged: 'I love you, boy.'

What else could a parent say to a child at that point – when protection wasn't an option, when pride didn't begin to cover it? What else was there to say really? Nothing except: *'This is my son, the Beloved, with whom I am well-pleased.'*

Beloved

Oh, how you love us, God –
number the hairs on our heads, count fingers and toes,
memorise the curve of our smile and the hope in our hearts.

Oh, how you love us, God!
You see the beauty housed within us
and you give it a home.
You're intimately familiar with our frailties,
but refuse to hold them against us.
When we are at our best,
we emulate you and adore each other.
When we are at our best,
we cannot help the love.
Thank you for the shelter we find with each other,
the freedom found in not having to pretend.
Thank you for the challenge laid at our door
when we are called to change our plans
for somebody else's dream.

Oh, how you love us, God –
when we are at our best,
we emulate you and adore each other.
Teach us to be at our best.
The world sometimes shows us its worst –
hunger, poverty, war, oppression, greed, injustice ...
When we are part of the worst the world has to offer,
stop us and change us and turn us back towards love.
Whenever and wherever we can,
help us to help each other.

Dancing in the desert

A meditation for the start of Lent

When I wonder if there's a God, I always look to the times when my soul wanted to whisper *'Thank you'* to someone. I mean, who do you thank for the contagious wee giggle of a five-year-old, or the way your children can crack your heart in half with just a smile?

Who do you thank for the lover who can still make everything OK, just by holding you; and what about all the folk who know you really well – and still love you?

When you look up and the sky is dripping with stars and your heart skips a beat at the beauty of it all, who hears your private *'Wow'* and smiles?

I don't wonder but that's God. 'Well-pleased', that's what God whispers to us now.

Listen. Take some time now to tell God what makes your heart sing. Feel free to whisper whatever you want to. It'll get where it needs to go …

Silence or quiet music …

Sometimes you just need to hear that you are loved; sometimes that's enough – sometimes that's everything.

As you take a deep breath and submerge yourself in the waters; as you rise wet and warned and welcome, prepared to walk into Lent, hear this:

> *You are loved by God.*
> *Each and every one of you:*
> *cherished, adored, liked –*
> *just as you are.*

God loves you,
Jesus loves you,
the Spirit loves you:
Three-in-One.
No exceptions.

Follow Christ's footsteps,
walk into the wilderness –
and dance in the desert.

Beloved of God,
come on a journey.

On fasting

Slow us down for the fast

Slow us down for the fast.

Still our restless spirits …
Calm our racing minds …
Centre our being …
Let our longing linger.
Let it take root
and create a beautiful yearning space
that has the time to ache …

Slow us down for the fast.

Silence the siren voices.
Wait for our weary wanting
to meet our need and find common ground …
Hold back the driving beat of our hearts
and let the drums of our internal wars fall silent …

Slow us down for the fast.

Before the journey begins …
Before the wanderlust calls us …
Before the wilderness beckons
and breaks our searching spirits …

Slow us down for the fast.

Confession is good for the soul

A call to worship for the start of Lent (from Psalm 32)

Happy are those whose transgression is forgiven, whose sin is covered.

CONFESSION IS GOOD FOR THE SOUL.

Happy are those to whom the Lord imputes no iniquity, and in whose spirit there is no deceit.

CONFESSION IS GOOD FOR THE SOUL.

While I kept silence, my body wasted away through my groaning all day long. For day and night your hand was heavy upon me; my strength was dried up as by the heat of summer.

CONFESSION IS GOOD FOR THE SOUL.

Then I acknowledged my sin to God, and I did not hide my iniquity. I said, 'I will confess my transgression to the Lord', and God forgave the guilt of my sin.

CONFESSION IS GOOD FOR THE SOUL.

Therefore let all who are faithful offer prayer to God.

CONFESSION IS GOOD FOR THE SOUL.
LET US WORSHIP GOD.

Prayer:

God of all,
we confess that we do not like to confess.

It makes us feel vulnerable,
it reminds us that we are fragile and flawed,
it calls us to admit to you, ourselves and others
that we need to change.

God of all,
we confess that we do not like to confess.
We ask for your forgiveness and your help because we know –
confession is good for the soul.

Assurance of pardon:

Fast comes the forgiveness.
Before the syllables have made a sound
your confession clears the way.
God holds no grudges,
so let go of your grief.
You are forgiven.

Hungry for the fast

We're hungry, Lord –
for time that isn't rushed or triple-booked,
for family and friends,
for a chance simply to be.
And we're starved sometimes:
for affection and understanding,
for love and peace,
for a moment to share.
We're hungry, Lord.

Sung response: 'God bless to us our bread' (Federico Pagura and John L. Bell, from *Love and Anger*, Wild Goose Publications; also in CH4, 763)

We're hungry, Lord –
for justice and freedom,
for equality and other folk's safety,
for a fair chance in this world.
The haves and have-nots never meet,
so how can they share?
Help us to bridge the gap
and satisfy the ones who need help to heal.
We're hungry, Lord.

Sung response

We're hungry, Lord –
for a new path,
a different direction,
a vision that you endorse.

Keep us searching for the bread of heaven,
which has the power to sustain us all.
Keep us hopeful as we fast, Lord,
because we know that you can fill us with
the food that keeps us satisfied.

Sung response

Aisles of endless options

Paper or plastic,
free-range or economy pack,
regular or supersize?
All these choices ...

Me or you,
us or them,
then or now,
yes or no?
All these choices ...

Stay or go,
shout or listen,
love or hate,
the hard slog or the easy option –
all these choices ...

Be with us, God,
because sometimes it would be so much easier
to not decide anything,

but simply float on a breeze of least resistance.
So much simpler to add our tacit assent
to what everyone else's conscience can live with.

But that's not good enough, and you know it.
You choose to infiltrate the places
we'd rather leave undisturbed,
because they're vulnerable, unstable –
likely to kick off and ruffle feathers.

You choose to open cans of worms,
stir up stale places –
you've even been known to change minds and ways –
how'd you ever manage that?!

Christ, stand in the aisles of our endless options
and tell us what you think;
write your reminders at the top of our
'oh so important' list of priorities.

All these choices ...
not everyone in the world has them:
we are so lucky and so laden.

When we choose,
let our hands and hearts reach towards you.
When we choose,
may we choose to put down some of what we have
to make room for what we need.

This or that?

This or that?
Me or them?
Now or later?
More or less?
You or it? …
Decisions, decisions, decisions ...
So what'll it be?

God be with us,
when we are so subtly asked
to choose between two masters …
God be with us.

God, who looks far down on the heavens and the earth,
help us to see what is right in front of us.
Help us to see that what is good for them is good for us all,
that later might be too late for some,
that less can so often mean more,
that the 'it' we look for so desperately is you …

This or that?
Me or them?
Now or later?
More or less?
You or it? …
Decisions, decisions, decisions ...
So what'll it be?

God be with us,
when we are subtly – so subtly –

asked to choose between two masters …
God be with us.
Amen

Giving up gossip

'Did you hear what he said?'

'Do you know what I heard?'

'Straight from the horse's mouth – and that's the gospel.'

God of us all,
forgive us when our mouths run ahead of the rest of us –
when we are only too quick to give our opinions
or our interpretations
or our version
instead of holding fire until our brains and hearts have a chance
to catch up with our tongues.

Forgive, when we assume we know what someone's like,
when we run to jump on the bandwagon of popular opinion,
when we are keen to think the worst
and ready to wade in, oar in hand.

Give us wisdom
to see through your eyes and hear through your ears,
to hold our tongues when they get ahead of us:
to love with your heart.

As a way to fast throughout Lent, give up gossip. Let go of listening to unkind words, and be attuned to how easy it is to use your words as weapons rather than tools.

Handiwork and heaven

Leader 1: Lord God, what do you see when you look down from heaven? When you consider the work of your fingers, the handiwork of your immense imagination, what do you see?

Leader 2: When you see our searching for you, our hopeful holding on – when you see some grace, thank you, because it has all come from the hope we find in you. Hear us, God of all – from the lips of infants and children, from adolescents and would-be adults, from folk in with the bricks and new friends never met; from all these, you have ordained your praise.

Leader 1: Lord God, what do you see when you look down from heaven? When you consider the work of your fingers, the handiwork of your immense imagination, what do you see?

Leader 2: When you see our searching for more things to fill the emptiness we feel, when you see our helpless holding on to stuff – when you see us so desperately clinging that our hands are too preoccupied to reach out to each other, help us. Remind us to be mindful that the world you have crafted is a gift to be shared out equally. When we take more than our share, give us grace to redress the balance. Help us to change: to look up into your heavens and call on your name and walk your new path. Show us again the hope that is in you.

Leader 1: Lord God, what do you see when you look down from heaven? When you consider the work of your fingers, the handiwork of your immense imagination, what do you see?

Leader 2: When you see things you never put in place; when you see your children warring and weighing options and wasting the world you so carefully created, teach us. Help us to hear our brothers and sisters when they cry, and open the eyes and ears of our hearts that we might see family, not 'foreigners'.

We pray this day for places where there is no justice, just violence. We pray this day for people who go hungry, while others have so much they wallow in complacency. We pray this day for folk who suffer. We pray this day that this day we might begin to be different. Amen

Prophet/profit

Leader 1: 'Blessed are the poor in spirit, for theirs is the kingdom of heaven.'

Leader 2: We don't want to be poor. Poor means needing things, poor means going without, poor means being afraid and having no safety net. How can you call that a blessing? Surely goodness and mercy and a financial cushion should follow us all the days of our lives.

Leader 1: 'Blessed are those who mourn, for they will be comforted.'

Leader 2: I think I'd rather just be comfortable. Mourning is messy; mourning is the way you feel when your mortality materialises and you realise you aren't going to be around forever. Then you have to decide what's really important. Comfortable is the truest comfort.

Leader 1: 'Blessed are the meek, for they will inherit the earth.'

Leader 2: Mice are meek and they inherit mousetraps or maybe a bit of somebody's leftover cheese, if they're lucky. No thank you to that. You have to stand up for yourself or you'll get flattened.

Leader 1: 'Blessed are those who hunger and thirst for righteousness, for they will be filled.'

Leader 2: Filled with what exactly? Last time I was hungry and thirsty I felt empty and weak. And standing on your principles is all well and good, but there are times when you have to go with the flow and compromise if you're going to keep up with the Joneses.

Leader 1: 'Blessed are the merciful, for they will be shown mercy. Blessed are the pure in heart, for they will see God. Blessed are the peacemakers, for they will be called sons of God.'

Leader 2: Yada, yada, yada – black sheep of the family more like. Don't listen to that claptrap, it'll only end in tears. If you look out for number one it won't matter what they call you.

Leader 1: 'Blessed are those who are persecuted because of righteousness, for theirs is the kingdom of heaven. Blessed are you when people insult you, persecute you and falsely say all kinds of evil against you because of me. Rejoice and be glad, because great is your reward in heaven, for in the same way they persecuted the prophets who were before you.'

Leader 2: Fine, you decide: Profit *(spells this out: P-R-O-F-I-T)*, or prophet *(spells this out: P-R-O-P-H-E-T)*. You can't have it both ways, so for God's sake decide …

Leader 1: Amen

On fasting

(Isaiah 55)

Voice 1: 'Everyone who thirsts, come to the waters; and you who have no money, come, buy and eat!'

Voice 2: Um, are you sure about that? I don't know if that's such a good idea. What if we run out? And what about those of us who've worked hard for what we have?

Voice 1: 'Come, buy wine and milk without money and without price.'

Voice 2: But what about the budget – what about savings? Don't you think we need to keep some of the stock in check?

Voice 1: 'Why do you spend your money for that which is not bread, and your labour for that which does not satisfy?'

Voice 2: Now you're not making sense. I'm trying to make sure that I spend carefully and save wisely. The future is uncertain – and I have to protect myself.

Voice 1: So who will protect the others? ...

The most important thing

What's the most important thing about you – when you strip everything else away, what's left? Let me help: what you own is gone; what you've worked so hard for has disappeared. Money, savings, property, knick-knacks and toys. And you stand around looking at the empty space. *(Sigh)* Imagine …

What's the most important thing about you – when you strip everything else away, what's left? Let me help: your family – that's gone. Your roots, your history, your community, the centre that you return to for validation, comfort, the witnesses to what you do every day no longer exist. And you stand around looking at the empty space. *(Sigh)* Imagine …

What's the most important thing about you – when you strip everything else away, what's left? Let me help: your accomplishments are gone – your resume, your education and qualifications, your experience and reputation. It's all … well, poof … And you stand around looking at the empty space. *(Sigh)* Imagine …

What's the most important thing about you – when nothing's left – when you strip everything else away and stand there vulnerable with nothing to hide behind?

Let me help.

Because of your hardness of heart

Hardness of heart has a lot of side effects ...
ends up that your heart's not the only thing affected.
Closed-mindedness,
that tends to happen too;
often it begins with a narrowing that gets progressively worse.
Tight fists sometimes manifest themselves
and that symptom can present itself when you're holding money,
or in extreme cases,
the tightening becomes clinching
and moves to bouts of violence.

So thank you, God, for love –
it is a powerful tonic,
if we're brave enough to swallow it.
It may be a bittersweet pill but it has quite an effect.

God of the soft and wide-open heart,
we ask that you help us to cure our ailing world.
The cure has to begin with a little self-diagnosis
so help us to re-evaluate our priorities and rethink our prejudices.
Help us to ask ourselves some different questions:
'What if that were me?'
rather than 'Shame on them'.
'What part have I played in the global mess?'
rather than 'Me and mine are fine, so all's right in my world'.

In your world, God, all are loved,
all are safe – all are yours.
Soften us to that way of being,

open us to that way of working,
loosen our grip on what we think we've earned
and help us see it as a gift that is only ours to share.

God of the soft and wide-open heart,
we ask that you help us to cure our ailing world.
The cure has to begin with a little self-diagnosis
so help us to love.
It is a powerful tonic,
if we're brave enough to swallow it.
Amen

Hold fast as we listen

Lord, we love to listen –
to a good word,
to the sound of laughter,
to a singing child,
or a whispering lover …

But Lord – we need help listening:
to the brokenhearted who need us to embrace them,
to the unlovely who need us to love them,
to the captives and prisoners who need release …
So, Lord, we ask you to help us hold fast as we listen,
and we ask you to listen now to our prayers …

We pray today for children who cannot speak for themselves,
and are treated as property to be bought and sold …

We pray for our brothers and sisters who are hungry,
while we have more than we need …

We pray for those who are sick in mind, body or spirit
and have no safety net,
while we worry about a waiting list …

We pray for our brothers and sisters in war-torn places
as they cope with devastation we cannot even begin to imagine …

We pray for peace in the hearts of those who find that anger,
disappointment, bitterness and fear have taken over everything …

And we pray for ourselves –
that we might hear your word when you speak to us
and that we might have the courage to follow
where you call us.
Amen

On slowing down

Glad you're here

Loosely based on Psalm 15

All you young folk,
energy pumping through your veins,
excitement and potential exuding from every pore,
managing to sit still, abiding in this sanctuary –
not as easy as it looks –
God is glad you're here.

All you grown folk,
experience trying to help you keep on an even keel,
energy tapped just a bit too often,
abiding in this sanctuary –
settling down in this place –
God is glad you're here.

All you older folk,
energy still yours, though measured,
experience showing you that there's always more to learn,
abiding in this sanctuary –
reflecting in this place on the life behind and before you –
God is glad you're here.

All of us are God's folk and we are welcome here.
Come, says Jesus, sit for a while.
Come, says Jesus, bide your time.
Come, says Jesus, and abide with me.

Let the sweetie wrappers be silent

A call to worship

I promise you that we will not pass our allotted time today – in an hour, you will be leaving this place. And with that assurance, I will now ask you a favour. We are going to begin with an offering …

Take off your watch, and when the usher comes to your seat, place it in the collection basket. Don't worry, it will be returned to you at the end of the service *(devise a system for this and explain it)*. Take out your day planners, your Filofaxes and palm-pilots and smartphones – the dumb ones too – and add them to the collection. Don't worry, you'll get them back too.

And lay aside the other things you may have brought to distract yourselves – paper for doodling, a wee bit of knitting … Let the sweetie wrappers be silent. This is God's time.

Choir sing 'Take this moment' (from One Is the Body, *John L. Bell, Wild Goose Publications; also in CH4, 501) while watches, etc are being collected.*

There is not much time in this world that is sacred. Set-aside time needs to be created, protected, cherished. This time together with God is important. So take this moment, use this time, create a space … and see where it takes you. Let us worship God.

Song: 'Take this moment'

I have promised you that we will not pass our allotted time today – in less than an hour, you will be leaving this place. And with that assurance, I will now ask you another favour. Put your listening ears on – forget about your watches, your day planners, your Filofaxes, your palm-pilots and smartphones – the dumb ones too … Lay aside the other things you may have brought to distract yourself – paper for doodling, a wee bit of knitting … Let the sweetie wrappers be silent. This is God's time. There is not much time in this world that is set aside, protected, cherished. So I ask you to take this moment, use this time, create some space … and see where it takes you. Put your listening ears on.

And while we're at it – there are probably some other things we need to put aside too … other things we may have brought to distract ourselves: forget your preconceived notions about how the real world works. Put down your prejudices.

Give over your goals and objectives, lay aside the status quo, the business as usual, the rationalisations that make compromising your principles more comfortable.

This is God's time – so throw open every window and every door by which God's word might reach you. Open your hearts, your minds and your spirits to whatever God has to say to you today …

The choice

Every moment of every day, we make decisions. Some so seemingly insignificant that we slip into their pattern without being conscious of it, but they begin to frame us, whether we realise it or not.

In one of my favourite quotes, C.S. Lewis says of choices: *'People often think of Christian morality as a kind of bargain in which God says, "If you keep a lot of rules I'll reward you, and if you don't I'll do the other thing." I do not think that is the best way of looking at it. I would much rather say that every time you make a choice you are turning the central part of you, the part that chooses, into something a little different than it was before. And taking your life as a whole, with all your innumerable choices, all your life you are slowly turning this central thing into either a heavenly creature or into a hellish creature' (from* Mere Christianity*).*

Every day there are choices to make – some so seemingly insignificant.

Will I scrape out of bed when the alarm clock goes off at 5am so I can be ahead of the game, or will I snuggle down under the duvet with the one I love and enjoy the peace together, before the mayhem of traffic, meetings and work?

Will I keep buying into the notion that I can buy happiness, or will I invest my time and money in people?

Will I spend an extra thirty minutes on the phone listening to my friend who is struggling, or will I screen the call, knowing that I'm running late?

Will I pause to pray or reflect or just sit in the stillness before I jump headlong into my day, or will I move ahead as though it all rests on me?

Will I put away my iPhone long enough to see the person standing in front of me or behind me in the queue at Sainsbury's or sitting next to me on the train?

And these are the easy choices, of course. But what are they turning me into? Which direction are they pointing me in? …

Slow me down, Lord.
Slow me down
and turn my soul back towards
the real me.

Stop for a minute

Wisdom calls from every corner of creation. Stop for a minute and listen to her. She'll whisper when the wind whistles through the trees; she'll sing, sounding suspiciously like birdsong; she'll wave to you from the grass that grows and the animals that graze and the people who grey.

God who lives with wisdom,
give the eyes of our hearts
insight to see you.
Attune the ears of our souls
to your eternal conversation.

Wisdom speaks through Christ our brother. Stop for a minute and listen to him … 'Love your enemy … forgive seven times seventy … become like a little child … do unto others as you would have them do unto you … give everything you have to the poor and come follow me … blessed are the peacemakers.'

Christ who lives with wisdom,
you taught not only through words but through action

and your life continues to pour into ours.
Give the eyes of our hearts insight to see you.
Attune the ears of our souls to your eternal conversation.

Prayer for a life below the surface

'How are you?'

'Trust you're fine.'

'All the best.'

'Hope you're well.'

'See you soon.'

'Just let us know if there's anything we can do.'

How easily those words trip off the tongue,
and how well they do their job sometimes –
keeping people at a respectable distance,
keeping the needs and hurts contained,
keeping us all safely on the surface.
We don't mean to, God,
but sometimes we're afraid to open the door to each other because someone just might need to come in.

Help us to hear ourselves when the word-walls begin to go up,
when niceties stop need in its tracks.
God, help us to hear each other.

It's good to talk

Jesus talked to everybody – not only talked, but listened. He learned about people: who they were ... what made them tick. And because he listened, really listened, he could help them. He could help them figure things out for themselves; he could help them turn around when they were headed in the wrong direction, and he could help them change.

So this morning, we're going to listen to each other a bit. And we're going to sing this in response:

Song: 'Our God is a God who makes friends', from *Sing with the World: Global Songs for Children*, John L. Bell and Alison Adam, GIA Publications

So, in twos or threes now, turn and tell your neighbour:

1. Something you've been thankful for this week.
2. Something you've been sorry about this week.
3. Something you've been worried about this week.
4. Something you'd like help with this week.

(Give folk a couple of minutes with each question, then begin singing 'Our God is a God who makes friends' again, inviting everyone to join in.)

On seeking Sabbath

'Anybody can observe the Sabbath, but making it holy surely takes the rest of the week.'

– Alice Walker, from *In Search of Our Mothers' Gardens*

Let us pray:

Remember the Sabbath day and keep it holy –
remember to set aside some time to listen,
to think about who I am
and who I want to be –
who you want me to be, God.

And it sounds like such a good idea,
until the deadlines loom
or you're trying to be in two places at once
or there are so many distractions to choose from.
Then we get busy and time flies!

Help us, God
to remember who we are and whose we are.
Help us, God –
to pay attention.

Jesus told stories

(An introduction to a story time)

Every day during Lent, your family, rather than giving something up, could instead read a book together.

Follow this simple liturgy at about the same time every day and create a space for being together and sharing stories. You could use a collection of short books or a Children's Bible.

Youngest child: What are we going to do now?

Adult: I'm going to tell you a story. Jesus told stories – great stories that made your mind open and your heart sing and your body itch to get out into the world and make things better. It's time now to hear a story like that.

Child: Why?

Adult: Because time is special, these stories are special – and you are special. OK?

Child: OK!

Slow river

Water under the bridge goes somewhere and waters places we haven't even dreamed of.

Old news is not just the wrapper for somebody's fish supper; it may have a longevity we underestimate. It could be part of a continued conversation that needs to be had.

Tied up, packed away, put to bed – finished off with a full stop at the end? One day is done, but another is on the horizon – we may have come to the end of a chapter, but the story is still being written. Instead of a full stop, life's story is always written with a comma.

Embrace the pause, fold it into your story.

The busy world rushes on

Beloved,
gather closer
for the days are closing in,
the hours are retreating
as the hush begins to call …

Gather closer
for the world is busy.
Silence yourselves and listen for God …

Be still, be calm,
as the day ends
and the night falls
and the busy world rushes on.

Take now for you … take now for God …
take now to think peaceably on the busy world
that rushes on.

Hush yourselves
and listen for God …

On reflection

Lent has begun

A call to worship

Voice 1: Lent is a time to search – to search for yourself. Who are you? Where are you going? Why? ...

Called out of the waters of your baptism and into the desert where you will face your desires, your dreams, your despair. Lent has begun, and it is time to search.

Sung response: 'Take, O take me as I am', by John L. Bell and Graham Maule, from *Come All You People*, Wild Goose Publications; also in CH4, 795

Voice 2: Lent is a time to take stock – to take stock of the life you are living, the goals you have set for yourself, the world you'll leave behind: will it be a better place because of your place in it? ...

Called out of the waters of your baptism and into the desert where you will face your past, consider your present, contemplate your future. Lent has begun, and it is time to take stock.

Sung response

Voice 3: Lent is a time to repent – to repent those wandering ways, those self-centred habits that have a hold on you, those hidden things you've buried away out of sight ...

Called out of the waters of your baptism and into the desert where you will find your way home again to God. Lent has begun, and it is time for the wanderer to come home again.

Sung response

Voice 1: It is time – time to summon out who you are meant to be. Lent has begun.

A reflection and meditation for the start of Lent

Meditator: I don't know how many of you have tried meditation – but it is not as easy as it looks! This is how it usually goes for me ...

Guide: OK, time to begin: Breathe in through your nose ... and out through your mouth ... in through your nose ... and out through your mouth.

Meditator: *(breathing in and out)* So far, so good.

Guide: Focus ... relax ... clear your mind ... don't let any extraneous thoughts cloud your space.

Meditator: *(breathing in and out)* This isn't so difficult. I can do this. No extraneous thoughts here. Oh, darn it, wait a minute. Technically speaking, thinking that you have no extraneous thoughts *is* an extraneous thought. OK – stop thinking!

Guide: No need to fight or thrash against the thoughts that come unbidden into your mind. Treat them as you would a dog on a leash: when they wander away, rein them in.

Meditator: OK, *now* you tell me ... reining in – here, girl ...

Guide: Breathe in through your nose ... and out through your mouth ... in through your nose ... and out through your mouth. Focus solely on your breathing: let that awareness completely saturate your thoughts, allowing yourself to enter a calm place where you can sit at peace with your spirit ... OK, I will count down from 5, and then leave you for two minutes in silence. 5,4,3,2,1 ...

Meditator: *(breathing sounds)* It's awfully quiet in here. (Stop thinking.) Sorry, but it is. (Could you knock it off?) Sorry ... Wonder what we're doing after this? (It doesn't matter – we're supposed to be saturated with the present, you goofus!) Oh yeah, but still, I wonder –

Do you feel that itch? It's right above our left eye. Can we scratch it? (No, we can't: we're supposed to absorb those feelings into our present state of calm and accept them.)

But it itches! If we just scratch it, then it'll disappear and maybe then we can re-enter our calm! And anyway, nobody's going to see. They're all meditating – with their eyes closed – get it? (I'm not going to have this conversation with you. Breathe. In through your nose ... and out through your mouth.) Do you smell onions? (We had onions for lunch. Shut up!)

Guide: OK, the two minutes is coming to an end.

Meditator: Damn it! (Thank goodness.)

Guide: Take your time coming back. There is no rush. I will count you back from five and when you're ready, open your eyes. 5,4,3,2,1 ...

Meditator: I don't know how many of you have tried meditation – but it's not as easy as it looks. Finding the focus, settling down at the beginning is fine. Trying to sustain it – that is something else completely. When it all gets quiet and you are left alone with yourself, it is amazing how noisy and distracting your self can be. Like so many things in life, the beginning is doable; remaining there, finishing it – that's an entirely different kettle of fish. Welcome to Lent. Blessings as you journey.

Meditation

Sit in the silence and drink in the unbidden sounds ... Let them wash over you like rain. Rarely is there nothing to listen for ...

Close your eyes and see the secret things dance – light and shadow ...

Rarely is everything darkness ...

With your eyes still closed, breathe deeply, in through your nose ... and out through your mouth ... breathe deeply ... exhale fully ... breathe in peace and calm ... blow out worry ...

And now, for the next few moments, breathe your prayers quietly to God, who will gather them up and know what to do ...

Listen

Voice 1: We've come to listen for the word of God ...

Voice 2: The still small voice ... the whisper to your heart, the silent stir in your soul ...

Voice 1: We're called to listen for the word of God ...

Voice 2: The crying child, the pleading mother, the distraught father ...

Voice 1: We're challenged to listen for the word of God ...

Voice 2: The new idea, the exciting but disturbing insight, the unlikely prophet ...

Voice 1: We're called to listen for the word of God ...

Voice 2: The world whispers, *'Listen, God is speaking. You don't want to miss this.'*

Why are you here?

Why are you here? What is so important to you that you've gathered here in the quiet of this church? What is so important to you – or maybe *who* is so important?

Here are some important people:

An unborn child whose future is down to her postal code ...

An overworked, disillusioned 40-something who can't make ends meet ...

A battered woman …

An imprisoned teenager …

An Ebola patient …

A young man in Gaza who'd like to see the world …

Here are some important people …

Family …

Friends …

Neighbours …

The person who sits near you in the pews on Sunday morning whose name you don't know …

Why are you here? What is so important to you that you've gathered here in the quiet of this church? What is so important to you – or maybe *who* is so important?

They are – all of them … And any other ones whose faces or plights or hopes and dreams flooded into your thoughts these last couple of minutes. They are why we are here. Because the Church is the Body of Christ, the family of God, and there is work to do. Because if we are to go out into the world, we, like Jesus, need to find space to pray and reflect: to collect our strength by gathering together in the quiet of this moment …

Letter by Gracie to Gracie

This is a school assignment written by my daughter Gracie. It is a letter to her younger self – wouldn't it be great if we could do this?

Dearest and most wonderful me,

I write you this letter to give you advice that may help you over the next two years of your life's journey, and also because Mr Fulton decided that it would be a good idea for us to write to our past-selves as they (you) start third year. I, on the other hand, feel that this is just another way for teachers to torture poor, lovely children during their summer holidays.

Anyhow, congratulations on reaching third year! I know last year was not the best year for us due to the misfortunate combination of glasses, hair-frizz, braces and being the new girl – definitely not a good combination. But it's all over and you can now look forward to a bright future which, with my help, can be even more spectacular than it would otherwise be: because you will have me to protect you from my past stupidity and to prepare you for some of the great, and not so great, experiences of your Standard Grade years – oh, don't I feel powerful right now!

First things first: we must remember that nail polish *does* in fact have an odour and, believe it or not, biology teachers do not enjoy the smell of acetone welcoming them to their rooms on a Monday afternoon. I'm sorry, sweetie, but they will not understand that you did not realise that the aroma would disturb the lesson. And they especially won't appreciate you pointing out that the only reason that you painted your nails in the first place was because they were late – it will not end well for you, even if it did happen to be true. Giving your skeleton a funny hairdo and naming it after the same biology teacher is also a big no-no!

Now, to be boring and clichéd – to repeat advice given by every adult you have talked to this summer – all your teachers, parents, grandparents, aunties, old ladies at the church and so on: you must revise from the start of third year to the end of fourth year. Little me, this means you need to revise continuously throughout the two years. Do not wait until the night before the exam to learn two years' worth of physics (actually, just don't take physics at all – it's a little bit evil). If you do, as I say, the embarrassment of crying on Mull in front of your entire family when you discover you got a 2 in History may be prevented; however, if you choose not to listen to this, embarrassment will be an inevitability. May I remind you that I am older, wiser, smarter and better than you, so do as I say.

Since we were little, we have marked the start of the year and got geekily excited about stiff new school bags and smooth new jotters yet to be marked by the doodled graffiti pushing past the margin and sneaking on to the page. (Yup, we still do it and still get in trouble for it. I am actually beginning to think we just don't learn!) In fact, we even measure the year in the number of jotters we can get through before the start of summer, but I want these next years to be different for you because I want you to really use this time and not just get through it: to realise how much you regret when it's over and there is nothing that can be done about it.

Jonathan Larson once pondered: 'How do you measure a year?' He came to the conclusion that you should measure your life in the lives of your friends, and this is something that will become very potent to you over the next two years. You will learn through all of your friends how important it is to live every day to its full and to take every opportunity you're given (if legal and not too harmful). You'll learn that life is too short not to. In the past few months I have wished more than anything that I had spent more time with people I cared about; that when times got tough I had not just folded in on myself, but that I had been more open and honest when people asked me how I was and trusted that they wanted to hear the truth, not just the automatic 'I'm fine' answer. You don't have to keep your feelings bottled up, scared to let people know the truth. I don't want you to be scared of letting yourself be vulnerable.

As I sit here on the Tuesday morning just before I leave for school, I remind us to change our ways, use our time wisely and never ever waste a minute (however, *EastEnders* is not wasteful). Hopefully having read this spectacular specimen of a letter, your next two years will be filled with happiness and smiley faces. Your days will be filled with the joy of freedom – here's hoping!

Love,

Us, me and you!

Gracie Foster-Fulton

Listen to the word

Jesus our brother,
you told stories that challenge our common conceptions –
they bend the rules, stretch our souls.
And the stories aren't a patch on the life you lived
and the love you poured out into this world.

Today, as always, you ask us to listen and to consider
whether we will follow your upside-down way.
So finely tune our ears to your wavelength.

Help us to 'Listen to the word that God has spoken'.

'Listen to the word that God has spoken.'

Jesus our brother,
there were a lot of things you said,
so much to remember.
Help us to hold fast to the important stuff;
strangely enough the important stuff
also tends to be the difficult stuff:
love your enemies,
pray for those who persecute you
(and that doesn't mean you pray for their defeat or destruction),
share your hard-earned, well-deserved things:
money, food, property.
Don't try to take over God's job and start judging others;
leave that to the only one capable
and get on with the task at hand –
loving your neighbour.
The globe has exploded and become a neighbourhood –

so there are lots of different kinds of people
to find a place for in our hearts.
You have called us to see the spark of God in every face –
to be faithful to your upside-down dream …
So finely tune our ears to your wavelength.
Help us to 'Listen to the word that God has spoken'.

'Listen to the word that God has spoken.'

Jesus our brother,
you told stories that challenge our common conceptions –
bending the rules, stretching our souls,
but they aren't a patch on the life you've called us to live.

The world needs your kind of love poured into it.
And so we pray for faithful love that leads to peace …
We pray for places in the news today:
places we've never heard of,
and places so familiar
as to be in danger of becoming background noise.
We pray for those who are hurting in mind, body or spirit;
we pray for the hungry and the homeless
and those who are held hostage to our greed.
Turn us upside down through your grace.
And when we hear your whisper calling us to consider
how faithfulness looks and feels today,
may we listen to the word that you have spoken.

'Listen to the word that God has spoken.'

Amen

Blessed are you

Blessed are you – a part of history, a piece of the puzzle, a thread in a much larger tapestry.

Blessed are you – a grain of sand on an endless white beach, a drop in the ocean, withering grass, fading flower – beautiful in your fleeting fragility.

Blessed are you – voice in a choir, instrument in a symphony, echo and harmony and counterpoint.

Blessed are you – star in a deep-blue universe, spinning in infinity, bound to a time.

Blessed are we – the centre of the universe isn't all it's cracked up to be. God knows that and so saves us from it. Bound to each other, go in peace.

On journeying

Doorway to the desert

Your breath moved over the waters of chaos:
blew life into stillness at the birth of the world.
Your heartbeat sings through the waters of each birth
and the wildness of the cosmos
and the wonder of insight.

Our feet stand at the doorway to the desert ...
we hold our breath,
our hearts skip a beat
and we take a first faltering step
into insight.

As Lent begins,
our hope is that we are able to wait with you in this time,
before you walk into the wilderness
and the work you came for begins.

Christ walks the road beside us

When we walk easily down a clear path, Jesus ambles along beside us, glad of the company.

CHRIST WALKS THE ROAD BESIDE US.

When we stumble along because the path is hard and the darkness is falling, our brother helps us find our way. We are never alone, because Jesus loves us.

CHRIST WALKS THE ROAD BESIDE US.

Whenever and wherever and however we go, Jesus walks with us. And we are called to walk the same way with our brothers and sisters, upholding each other.

CHRIST WALKS THE ROAD BESIDE US.

The net prayer

You ask us to follow you –
to leave our nets and come on a journey …
but to be honest, we've got so tangled up, God –
in the things we want,
in the half lies we tell, so subtle
that we've even managed to convince ourselves of them.

And nets are strong things – they're meant to hold,
designed to trap.
They can snag you before you even know what's happened.
And nets are alluring –
it's so easy to depend on them to help us get
what we think we need.

So help us, God:
give us the courage to cast our nets aside
and follow you on our journey;

to seek wisdom that helps us see
the snares for what they are;

to learn the hard difference between
what we want and what we need,
so that we catch and keep our share
but no more than that.

Deep and wide and wonderful is your world, God –
free us to find that out.
Amen

Going against the tide

'I will follow you wherever you go.'
That's what your first friends said
and that is what we here hope to do.

But sometimes it's a little stormy where you are.
Doing what's right can stir things up a bit,
going against the tide can make waves
and though you called to the wind and the waves in a story once,
they always seem to come back to blow again.

But maybe, Jesus, we need to look deeper
into the lake our boat sails on ...
maybe you promise a different calm:
not troubles ceasing and all answers given
and everything black and white,
and life gliding on the smooth glass of perfection,
but a sense of abiding peace
such as the world cannot give.

So, Jesus, on the days when the sun shines and the birds sing
and it's our day,
help us to get in the boat with you.

If you want to get to God

'The way, the truth and the life – if you want to get to God, that's how.'

That's what you said, Jesus … but which way? All these paths to choose from – all these ways to go. Tell us again, Jesus: about forgiving our enemies and sharing our bread and laying down our weapons.

Tell us again about the path to peace, the freeway of forgiveness, about journeying with communal supplies. The way can be hard, but it gets you to God. Walk the way with us, Jesus.

'The way, the truth and the life – if you want to get to God, that's how.'

That's what you said, Jesus … but which truth? There are so many versions, so many sincere voices assuring us they can be trusted, so many face values to conjure with. All these conflicting truths …

Tell us again, Jesus, about the speck in our eye, the child's Kingdom; tell us your upside-down stories about unlikely good Samaritans and beloved prodigal sons. Tell us the Truth, Jesus, over and over again. It will get us to God.

'The way, the truth and the life – if you want to get to God, that's how.'

That's what you said, Jesus … but which life are you talking about? The successful one where we meet everybody's expectations? The good life where we collect the most stuff? The exciting life where we chase our dreams and seize the day before our threescore years and ten end?! So many lives we could lead, so which one?

Tell us again, Jesus, about the lilies of the field and the birds of the air, remind us that we are salt and light, tell us again about laying down our life for a friend.

The way, the truth and the life – you walked the way, you told the truth, you lived your life so that we could be free. If we want to get to God, this is how – that's what you keep saying, Jesus. Help us hear you and follow on.

'I am the way, the truth and the life – if you want to get to God, that's how.'

A question for Yahweh

Yahweh, the great I AM, humanity has a question – asked over and over and over again … What is this life?

Breathing in and out, heart pumping, atoms multiplying, synapses and neurons firing? …

What is this life? Maybe it's time – seconds to minutes to hours to days – days to weeks, months, years? …

What is this life? Accumulating insight, collecting toys? Doing good, doing no harm – what is this life?

We need to know, God, because the one we want to follow has told us that the best way to save our life is to lose it – so we need to know exactly what's at stake here. What do we need to lose, and is it worth the trade-off?

Yahweh, the great I AM, humanity has a question – asked over and over again … What is this life?

As we set out in search of answers, keep asking us the question. Stay with us in our searching.

When we sense something other than ourselves in all this, stir that sense into insight that moves us towards each other, for in loving each other, we may find answers that elude us.

Forgive us when we fail; lift us when we fall; turn us towards holy ground where we can take off our sandals, put down our burdens and feel the warmth of the sand; where we can feel the solid earth beneath our feet and the freedom of our spirit as it stretches towards yours.

The time for searching has begun, and the journey itself is holy ground.

Sight and sound

'Journey with me,' says Jesus. 'Step away from safety and search a while in unfamiliar spaces. Listen and learn … Steal away and see.'

Wandering Word,
when we listen to voices that offer the easy option,
sing your love song to us again.

When we cannot see you because
we've put on the blinkers of self-service,
broaden our vision.
Nothing blocks our view like a narrow mind
or a twisted, biased perspective.

Give us insight, God,
to see you and hear you
and recognise you.
Breathe your peace into our hearts,
unstop our ears
and open our eyes.

God's children

I ranted on Tuesday morning – I probably raved a little too. And if I'd bothered to pay attention, I would have seen my eight-year-old daughter's eyes glaze over in boredom before I reached even the third sentence of my tirade. I felt perfectly justified in my tantrum – she was being incredibly silly, and she'd waited until we were almost out the door for school to get that way.

'I can't wear this stupid skirt – everybody'll laugh at me. It's not a proper skirt anyway because it's got legs in it – they'll call me a boy ... and you named me Alex, that's a boy's name. So this short, skirt-thingy will just prove it ... You've ruined my life.'

I stared, dazed for a moment by the force and passion with which she had managed to utter this drivel. Then I, on an equally adult note, launched into my own speech:

'Don't be so unbelievably stupid. That is the most ridiculous thing I've ever heard of ... It's called a "skort", because it looks just like a skirt. Nobody is going to even notice, and even if they did, what's the big, hairy deal! If someone is sad enough to make fun of your skirt because it's not exactly what everybody else is wearing, then that says more about them than it does about you. If your friends were all jumping into a fire, would you jump too?

Don't be afraid to stand out from the crowd – to be an individual ... Come on, Alex, pick up your school bag, wipe your face and let's get moving.'

Now, I'd like to tell you that she understood the error of her ways, that she marched proudly into her Primary 4 class determined to be a trendsetter and ready to make the world a better, safer place for all the kids forced to suffer oppression and bullying like she had, but I'd be a liar. Responding to my rant in the most predictable way imaginable, she stood hunched with her shoulders over her ears, warding off all my sage-like comments with the grace of a professional boxer. And when I made the mistake of stopping for breath, she set up an impressive counter-attack, wailing and crying at a volume and pitch designed to shatter glass and call all the dogs in the street to our door. Unprepared for this audial onslaught and coming dangerously close to being late for everything, I grabbed the 'real skirt' that had been lying in a crumpled heap on her bedroom floor for two days, doused it with air freshener, slammed the iron over it, tossed it to her and hissed: 'Put it on!'

I was exhausted, and stood piously leaning on the kitchen counter, tapping my foot, looking at my watch, counting to ten and practising level breathing between frustrated gulps of coffee, while Alex grumped into her skirt, mumbling something about 'another planet' and 'feeling sorry for her father' ... I looked down and saw my five-year-old looking up at me with the face of a saint. She held my hand, looked over at Alex to make sure she was paying attention, and said: 'Don't worry, Mummy. I don't mind wearing embarrassing things for you.'

We managed to get to school just as the last bell was ringing, and I, trying to put this unpleasant little melodrama behind us, said cheerfully, 'I love you girls' ... 'I love you too, Mummy ... You're the best Mummy in the whole world,' said Sarah Grace ... 'Yeah – whatever,' said Alex.

You know, I have two endings to my story: the imaginary one – the one that came like a cloud in my mind as I drove to school that morning; and the real ending, which came – as life does – full of surprises and beauty. Which one would you choose? …

The imaginary ending:

As I was pulling wearily into the parking space, Alex's friend Emma came running up the path shouting excitedly to us: 'Good morning, Mrs Fulton. Hi, Alex. Look at this new skirt I got yesterday … It's a "skort" … You know – skirt and shorts all together!'

I smiled sweetly at Emma, blew a kiss to Alex and drove away. 'Life is good,' I sighed.

The real ending:

As I was wearily manoeuvring my car out of the parking space, I looked up to see Alex and Sarah Grace bumping up the path ahead of me, Alex trying to look cool and nonchalant – despite her earlier battle with peer pressure, and Sarah Grace struggling to keep up with the only peer she cared about trying to impress … And then as I watched, Sarah Grace lost the battle with her oversized school bag and rather predictably squealed after Alex, who, to my surprise, stopped, sighed and took her hand. I felt my heart skip a beat before it lodged in my throat, but before I could manage a wee tear they turned and bellowed sweetly, 'Come on, Mummy, you've made us late!' Life is good, I sighed, as I drove away.

Prayer:

God leaps and dances,
limps and puts an exasperated hand
across a frustrated face.

God stifles a smirk when we are absolutely ridiculous,
and God's heart goes right into God's throat
at the beauty God sees in us.

We are God's children –
in all that we are …
If we live in that love,
then our life is a journey towards better …
not perfect,
but always on the road.

Jesus said, 'Let the little children come to me
and do not forbid them,
because the kingdom of God belongs to such as these.'
Not perfect – not angelic –
not meek always,
mild always,
but children –
so much like yours and mine –
so much like you and me.

Follow me

'Follow me', we hear you calling, God,
but that is such a journey.
Sometimes we have to go over old ground,
trudging back to the wrong turns we made
and retracing our steps.
That can mean we have to admit to the times
we should have asked for directions,
and to the times we decided on a shortcut
that turned out to be a dead end.
Going over old ground is not a popular tourist destination.

'Follow me', we hear you calling, God,
but that is such a journey.
Sometimes we have to venture into new territory,
choosing paths we can't be sure of.
We can't see over the tops of the hills or around bends
until we've travelled a long way on them,
and there are usually bumps and blocks in the road too.
Some places are so new that the satnav wouldn't even work,
so what do you expect us to do when we come to a crossroad?

Following you calls us to journeying, God,
so give us the determination we need –
courage when we stumble,
light in the darkness,
friends to point the way
and our own inner ear to follow the voice
we hear calling us home.

It is Lent and we hit the highway of self-reflection.
On our journey with you
we will meet a lot of interesting people.
The most surprising may just be the real us,
so keep us going, God.

Guide the steps of our hearts

'Come and follow me',
that's what you ask us to do.
To lay down the things that won't last,
that can't save,
that don't really matter.
But it's hard because,
to be honest,
we like our things;
we feel safe where we are.
And it's confusing:
How do you decide what to put down
and what's worth keeping?

God, who asks us to follow,
guide the steps of our hearts.
Help us to be brave enough to trust,
kind enough to care,
wise enough to consider the implications
of our actions and our omissions.
Forgive us when we follow the whims of fashion
instead of fashioning our lives after you.

Forgive us when we depend on things to make us happy,
when we ignore others because
to pay attention
might make us feel for them
and then we'd have to change.

'Come and follow me.'
That's what you ask us to do.

Help us to hear your call
and answer.
Amen

Where Jesus stays

Isaiah 49:1–7, John 1:29–42

You can tell a lot about a person by seeing where they stay, where they make themselves at home: where they are totally and completely themselves. I always think it's funny that a lot of the time when I feel really akin to someone, and then visit their home, I find out that there are things we have in common that are kind of 'in with the bricks'. For example – for some reason that would probably become instantly understandable if you popped in unannounced to my home – I become immediately uneasy, nay, suspicious, when I visit a home that is completely tidy. It makes me nervous. My friends euphemistically refer to my house as 'lived in'. And if there aren't dog toys, stray homework, opened mail and a glory hole stuffed with hidden treasure then I can't really relax! Yet I know there are people who feel that this is unacceptable in the extreme! That there is a place for everything and everything has its place.

I remember going to a dinner party at a friend's home (she will remain nameless) and she actually dropped to her knees in front of guests and combed out the fringe of her oriental rug. This was after having us all remove our shoes to protect said rug from any traces of dust.

As I said, you can tell a lot about a person by seeing where they stay, where they make themselves at home: where they are totally and completely themselves. It helps us get a handle on what makes folk tick, who they really are. If we pay attention, it may help us to respect them more and treat them the way they'd like to be treated. After all, who's to say what's weirder: combing out your oriental carpet, or having six months' worth of odd socks stuffed in a pillowcase under your dresser in case the others suddenly reappear looking for their 'sole' mate?

In our Gospel story this morning, we have what at first seems like a straightforward question, 'Where are you staying, Jesus?' But, as we've just discovered, there is more to it than that. 'Where are you staying, Jesus?' 'Come and see.'

I am intrigued by this story, drawn in and disturbed by it. What a question. What a profound theological opening. 'Where are you staying, Jesus?' Not 'where are you temporarily laying your divine head or what friends are putting you up and supporting you right now?' But 'where are you staying in the deepest sense of the word?' Where do you make your home, where are you totally and completely yourself? Or even further: on what will you refuse to move, where will you doggedly remain – steadfastly holding on, standing your ground; what mast are your colours nailed to? And he does not answer in any conventional way, but according to the Gospel of John says: 'Come and see.'

And I am intrigued, because after staying with him, these first disciples come away and say they have found the Messiah. They have named him and nailed their colours up there with him. They may not always follow, they may even betray him, but they have seen him for who he is. So, what did they see that made them feel so akin?

'Come and see' or, as it is literally translated, 'come to see'. This is a common, well-known rabbinical statement, and not an answer – but an invitation to explore. So, what did they see when they went to where he stayed? Not in the broad surface sense, but in that deeper place John invites us to go. I think Jesus was probably where he is now. Because there are places he will always stay.

I think Jesus is always going to be with the poor, holding them up in front of us, pleading their case – reminding us that the clichés and excuses and manoeuvres we have become so good at using are just that, and that he will never leave their side. If we choose to come and see where he stays, then we will have to put up with the poor always being there. 'Blessed are the poor ... when you do it to the least of these, my brothers and sisters, you do it to me.' The rich man and Lazarus, the eye of the needle. That's where he stays.

I think he'll always be on the side of peace. Even when we've done everything we can possibly think of to avoid conflict, Jesus is going to be there begging us all to reconsider, reminding us of the ones who died before because they couldn't find a way out. He is going to stay there hanging on to peace. 'Blessed are the peacemakers and the meek ... forgive seven times seventy ... Father, forgive them for they know not what they are doing.' That is where he stays. Throughout history, the Christian church has marched off to war and sometimes even used his name in vain as an excuse or reason, but that is not where he stays.

I think Jesus stays in the grey areas: 'come and see' not 'I know the answer, let me tell you.' He stays in the awkward, contentious questions that we face today in society – he stands smack dab in the middle of stem cell research and nuclear power and global warming theories. He boldly invites us to examine what we do, how we do it, whether we should do it just because we can. He frustratingly calls us with that same offer we heard in John's story: 'Come to see.' But come to see with me – always with me.

Journeying prayer

Speak to us again, old friend –
about first steps on a journey,
about packing the things that will last,
about travelling light –
not becoming weighed down by the things that seem important,
but are inevitably burdens and excess baggage.
And when we don't listen,
remember we're still learning,
and gently call our names once more.

Walk with us again, old friend –
through the past that can help us,
if we pay attention to the lessons of history,
into the present that needs our attention,
and into the future,
which depends on us.
And when we wander off or run away,
remember we're still learning,
and gently guide us back to you.

On new perspectives

Perspectives

Funny thing about perspectives:
you have to move to see a different one.
If you don't climb the mountain,
you can't view the plain.

New day dawning

Brand-new, blank-sheet, clean-slate, twinkle-in-the-eye idea
not yet formed.
A new day is dawning,
but it will be informed and impacted by your yesterday.

As you gaze over the vista that stretches before you,
remember the steps that brought you here.
As the light plays on the horizon of new insight,
revisit the paths that have led you,
the voices that have called you,
the hands you've held.
Carry them on, not as a burden to bear
but as guardians to guide you.
Step on into your new day dawning.
Life, love, lessons –
building blocks and brand new
and bringing us on.

Change have to get …

I tell stories about my grandmother a lot. She lived with us while I was growing up; our garage and playroom had been converted into a flat for her, so she was literally just a call away. Both my parents worked, so when we were sick, we stayed home with Granny and she'd make us soup, leave the 7-Up bottle open so the bubbles would flatten out and not hurt your stomach, and she'd whisper when you had a headache, and give you cool cloths if you were feverish. But, it was not quite the cushy number you'd imagine. She'd also quickly suss a faker and then you weren't allowed out of bed. If you were sick enough to stay home, you were sick enough to stay put; television, apparently, would hurt your eyes if you had a fever, so you weren't allowed to watch – and if you complained about boredom, well, she'd been a teacher all her working days, so she could sort you out with some practice sheets – maths were her favourite.

This is the woman who taught us to solve our disagreements as children in a wonderfully imaginative way: if we had a spat or an argument and came to her to sort it, she would have us sit on the back stoop and hold hands until we could come up with a solution ourselves or apologise to each other. We spent hours on that stoop, but we learned to compromise!

My granny also had a way of helping you see things a different way. When we hit her with the usual complaints: 'I have to go to school', 'I have to do my homework', 'I have to eat that for dinner?', 'I have to go to bed now?!' … she would say 'Change *have* to *get*' – and it used to drive us crazy! But it stuck, and you couldn't help but think it when you started to moan about all you had to do: think of the people who didn't get the opportunity to do the things you took so much for granted that you even moaned about them!

So, 'I have to go to school', 'I have to do my homework' became 'I *get* to go to school, have an education – a future.' 'I have to eat that?' became 'I *get* plenty to eat, and more!'; and 'I have to go to bed now?!' became 'I *get* to go to sleep in a safe, warm house and wake up with a brand-new day ahead of me.'

It didn't always work, but I'm fifty years old and I still hear her voice in my head and, on a good day, in my heart, where the real changes happen: 'Change *have* to *get*'.

When we're wrong, right us

I vividly remember my first 'sin'.

I don't much like that word, but I call it that and remember it that way, because I knew it was wrong and I willfully, and might add skilfully, did it – that's what made it grown-up, bona fide and well-worth remembering.

I was seven years old, and I stole Fran Marshall's ice cream. She'd been called to the head teacher's office at lunch, and her ice cream was still on her tray – uneaten. Nobody was watching, lunch period was almost over and that ice cream would probably just go in the bin – what a waste!

Fran had finished the rest of her lunch – she didn't need any ice cream – it wasn't like she was going to starve!

All of these thoughts came flooding into my brain, and I did it … I stuffed a paper napkin into my empty ice cream tub, and put the lid back on. When I was sure no one was looking, I switched the tubs and ate the evidence. About thirty seconds before the bell rang, Fran came back. She went straight for her ice cream. She opened the tub and when her face fell, my stomach sank.

Nobody'd been watching, lunch period was over, the empty ice cream tub got thrown into the bin … She was really sad, she didn't starve but she didn't get any ice cream either … all of these thoughts flooded into my brain; I felt awful. When I started to cry, my teacher decided I was sick and sent me home to my mum. And then I confessed.

I think we all remember a time like this: the first time we ever consciously did something we knew full well was wrong. And all of the rationalisations and excuses and human ducking and diving we do doesn't make a blind bit of difference in the cold light of day. We were wrong …

God, when we are wrong, right us –
give us the courage to look in the mirror of self-reflection
and straighten out what we see.

A mind is a terrible thing to waste

Genesis 11:1–9, 1 Corinthians 12:12–14

We've heard it said
and know it to be true
that a mind is a terrible thing to waste,
but I don't know where we got it into our heads
that it was somehow wrong to change it.

God forgive us when we are more interested
in defending our corner
than throwing light into it;
forgive us when the status quo is all we strive for –
a short walk indeed!
Forgive us when we have a sit-down strike
right in the middle of your moving day.

God of this bright new world,
when you give us new ideas,
when you open the world to a new understanding,
when you push and stretch in that eternal way of yours,
give us flexibility and grace
and a burning desire to be moved and grown with you.
Take away our fear of the future we cannot fathom,
and temper our love of 'what is' with a taste for
'what might be'.

God of love,
when a truth confronts us and guides us towards a new way,
help us to embrace it in your spirit,

and move with you wherever you live and move
and have your being.

God of the eternal stretch,
take us with you.
Grow us grand!
Amen

What makes me me

(A reflection for Transfiguration Sunday)

6:30 on a Friday morning – there wasn't one word written and there was a noticeable lack of inspiration. It was the end of a really hectic week; most of the time I seemed to be running from one place to another – usually timing it perfectly so I got rained on. The last few days seemed a blur of meeting rooms and trains, indoors to street-level, putting my head down and trudging from A to B – then getting back home and collapsing, waking up to an insistent alarm and starting all over again!

I craved calm, but the piece wasn't going to write itself, so I dragged myself up early, put the coffee on, lifted the laptop and headed into the living room. By 7:30, I'd drunk two cups of coffee and written an equal number of words. My husband, Stuart, came down, announced he was off to the gym and reminded me that it was my turn to walk the dogs. Hhh! I ignored him, mumbled something distinctly noncommittal; he sighed and rolled his eyes, but exertion beckoned so he grabbed his keys and went off to be healthy.

By 8:00, I had three words. As I dragged myself into the kitchen for my third cup of coffee, the dogs followed me, looking judgemental. Clara went over and stood by the leads; Lizzie went to the front door, scraping it with her paw and looking back at me. I tried a diversionary tactic, letting them out the back, but they knew that trick by now, so they headed me off and both went to the front door and started barking. I admitted defeat, went upstairs and just out of spite took a pair of Stuart's favourite socks.

I'd just walk them round the park, that'd do it – but the morning was surprisingly fresh and crisp so I was seduced and headed past the park and into the woods, up the spine towards the Wallace Monument. As we hit the path, I unclipped the leads and the dogs tore off in search of some elusive scent in the air. I kept on the path to the overlook at the top. The morning was clear as a bell – a bright blue sky let you see for miles. I looked down over the view: cattle dotted the field, there was a solitary rower on the river and the water was a flat shiny mirror snaking round Cambuskenneth with the ruins of the abbey standing guard. Looking ahead across the city, you could see the castle, the wind farm further on … I turned towards Dunblane. I could see Lecropt Church and the mountains – and I knew that the parish was nestled down there, tucked away – it made me smile. Over and just a bit below I could pick out my house, my bright yellow car in the drive. It was breathtaking up here.

I looked round at my blissfully happy companions, *maucket* now, having taken the opportunity to roll in the muddy grass – filthy smiling dogs, fresh cold air to breathe in, blue heaven for miles … I felt me coming back to myself and I have to say that me, myself and I, in truest Trinitarian fashion, did not want to leave each other but would have been content to stand and gaze all day at who and what stretched out before us/me. But, like we all know deep down, what made me me was waiting back down the hill. I needed that change in perspective – I needed to see the bigger picture in order to remind myself of that. So I gathered the dogs and myself together and ambled down the hill – the day, and me, transformed.

The Sunday before Lent is Transfiguration Sunday, when we are given the strange, powerful, symbolic story where Jesus is transfigured – where he stands with the Law embodied in Moses and the prophets personified by Elijah, and the voice of God says: *'Listen to him.'*

Before we begin our journey to Easter, we, his modern-day disciples, join Peter, James and John and are given a glimpse of the bigger picture, before we are asked to go back into that world and take the transformational message of his life and transfigure our lives and the world with it. This story appears in all three of the Synoptic Gospels, Matthew, Mark and Luke. All three want us to understand something about the Jesus who transfigures on the top of that mountain: he doesn't stay there and he never intended to and he doesn't expect us to either.

Lent offers us an opportunity to explore our lives, to climb to that change in perspective, to see the shining Saviour Jesus, who calls us back into the world he loves to hear God's voice saying: *'This is my son, the Beloved, with whom I am well-pleased – listen to him.'* Listen and learn – and love – and then go live differently.

Dreamer God

Sheltering, soothing God,
who calms the siren noises that batter our souls,
thank you for the different love song you sing in our world.
You dream so much bigger than we do –
of a world where things don't count as much as people,
where success isn't measured in money,
where time becomes something to share.

God our shelter,
for your gentle reminders,
for the love song you sing through our days,
for the times we catch the hint of your melody
and it turns us towards you,
thank you.

Vibrant vision of peace,
who takes us to a vista and whispers:
This is how it could be …
thank you for the different picture you paint.
You dream so much bigger than we do –
of a world where strangers are just friends we haven't met yet,
where difference is a cause for celebration,
where peace is the reality we all work for,
not a pipe dream for the naive.

God our vision,
for your constant reminders,
for the glimpses we catch of the world you want –
for the vistas that open to us, that beckon us

to follow your path,
we thank you.

Hospitable Lord of hosts,
whose love for the whole world cannot be quelled,
thank you for the rich feast you offer us.
You dream so much bigger than we do –
of a party table set buffet-style where the poor are first in the queue,
where everybody having enough is more important
than me having more,
where righting systemic injustice does not get confused with charity.

God our host,
for your persistent reminders,
for the way you call all to the table and then call us to share,
for the love your love opens in us,
we thank you.

God who dreams so much bigger than we do,
we pray for ... *(prayers of concern ...)*

God who dreams so much bigger than we do –
help us to learn that no one will be truly satisfied
until everyone is fed.
Amen

'Am I disturbing you?'

'Am I disturbing you?' that's what you say to us, God …
And then you ask us to move over,
or to pass some of what we have on down the line.

'Am I disturbing you?' you say,
as you clear your throat and gently enquire
whether we intend to speak up or not;
whether we intend to step up or not.
That's the way it is with you –
and on a good day, we're thankful for the push.

Keep on disturbing us, God.
When we are tempted to plod on towards the same old things –
when the false gods of money, success, comfort become the goals,
throw our routines out of kilter.
Keep on disturbing us, God.

The world needs some shaking up –
violence has become commonplace
and doesn't even have the power to shock us into sense.
Sometimes we even see it as sensible –
how frightening!
Images of hunger and poverty move us,
but only for a moment.
We sigh wistfully, nod sagely and go back to sleep – how sad!

If apathy has become a habit, help us break it.
We pray that when we hear your call to love,
we will take it seriously,
turn around
and embrace the change.
We pray that we will not just say our prayers,
but live them.
We pray that we will work for peace like people
who believe it's really possible.

'Am I disturbing you?' you say.
Please do, God.
Amen

Shrove Tuesday

All-age service for Shrove Tuesday

Making and sharing pancakes

For this service you will need water and a spray of heather; and a large bowl, mixing spoon, or whisk, and the ingredients to make pancake batter: flour, salt, milk, eggs. Gather in a circle in the crossing or in another central space.

Call to worship:

Life is a journey. We're always heading out to new things – new experiences, new people, new lessons to learn. Today, we're gathering to get ready for Lent, a special time to think about what kind of people we want to be – what kind of people God calls us to be.

Take the hand of the person next to you … feel the warmth and the strength. God gives us each other to love, and when we travel with each other – even though the path is bendy sometimes and we can't see over the next hill – it's easier to find our way.

Now let go of your neighbour's hand, and take a step back: make the circle wider. Imagine all the people who need love – maybe they're hungry or sad or scared or lonely, maybe they'd just like to be included or listened to. And now, in your imagination, bring *them* into the circle …

Let's have a prayer:

The journey into Lent begins tomorrow, God.
We've gathered with our friends to think about
where our lives need to go.
Thank you for always watching over us.
Help us to remember that we do not walk alone.
Amen

Journey to the font (place of baptism):

Life is a journey, and this afternoon we're going to hear a little bit about where our journey begins in church, so we need to move to the font (place of baptism).

> *Note for leaders:* If the font is near the church entrance, talk about the symbolism of it at the entry to the church; in some churches you could speak about the symbols carved on the font. If you use a bowl of water in the middle of the church for baptisms you could talk about welcoming a baby into the midst of the church family. If you baptise by immersion, speak about the symbolism of that.
>
> Talk about Jesus' baptism – giving him strength for the trials of the desert and the assurance he was loved: our baptism gives us strength for our journey and tells us that we are loved by God.

Bible reading: Matthew 3:13–17, Mark 1:9–11 or Luke 3:21–22 (Jesus' baptism)

A reminder of our baptism:

Offer a reminder of baptism (demonstrate on a volunteer first): Dip a spray of heather, or a similar plant, into the water and then sprinkle each person who comes forward, saying: *'God loves you. You belong in God's family.'*

Journey to the communion table/making pancakes:

Life is a journey, and this afternoon we're thinking about getting the strength to walk together, so we need to journey to the communion table.

The communion table is spread with the ingredients for pancakes.

Leader:

So why do we make pancakes on Shrove Tuesday? Let's listen …

Voice 1: Lent is the period of six weeks leading up to Easter. It starts on Ash Wednesday and ends during Holy Week. It lasts a total of forty days, not including Sundays.

The idea of Lent started in the fourth century – a long time ago. Back then baptisms took place on Easter Day. The forty days of Lent gave folk time to prepare for their baptism, and often they fasted: went without food to help them think about what they were about to do. Other members of the church would fast too.

Gradually Christians began to associate the fast with the 40 days when Jesus went into the desert to fast and pray in preparation for his ministry.

The day before Lent starts is Shrove Tuesday. We also call it Pancake Day. Traditionally Christians gave up meat, fat, eggs and dairy products for Lent. (Today people often give up things like chocolate and alcohol.) This was the last chance to use up these foods before Lent began. So, in preparation for Lent and Easter, let's mix up some pancake batter – and share pancakes!

Mixing the pancake batter:

At appropriate places, the readers call for help from the children.

Reader one: Today we make pancakes, and we think about the mix. We come to God as we are: some bits good, some bits bad. We're not always sure what is right and what is wrong – we're here together in a mixture called life.

Reader two: So we sift in some flour, smoothing out the lumps and bumps: the things we regret and the wrong things we've done. *(Action) …*

Reader one: And we add a dash of salt, to make the ordinary better – with God's love. *(Action) …*

Reader two: And we mix in some milk, because we all need strength for our journey with God. *(Action) …*

Reader one: And we add an egg, symbol of new life, and look forward to new possibilities. *(Action) …*

Reader two: We mix it all together, using up the ingredients of the past to give us the energy to move on towards the future, as we journey together through Lent to Easter.

(At this point all the children can be invited to come and help stir the pancake batter. Take your time, don't be afraid to be messy – have fun!)

Song: 'Today is Shrove Tuesday' (Tune: 'Streets of Laredo')

Today we remember that God always loves us.
Today we remember that here we belong.
Today we were splashed from a (font, bowl, etc) full of water.
Today is Shrove Tuesday, and this is our song.

Today we ask Jesus to help us be loving.
Today we make pancakes to help us grow strong.
Today we eat pancakes with chocolate and syrup.
Today is Shrove Tuesday, and this is our song.

Repeat verse 2

Prayer to send us on our way:

Voice 1: God, may this food we share give us strength
to survive in the tough times:
may we walk on into Lent ready to face
whatever comes our way.
God, may we never forget all those in the world
who are hungry, our sisters and brothers in ...
God, give us hunger for justice –
and for more of your good stuff!

Voice 2: God, as we eat these pancakes,
help us to remember that it's the mix and variety
that makes life really interesting –
different people, different experiences, different views ...
So help us to choose our pancake toppings with
a spirit of adventure,
experimentation and fun.
Amen

Blessing

Folk share pancakes in a nearby hall or community centre.

Sally Foster-Fulton and Ruth Burgess

Undivided attention

Leader 1: God calls us to Lent to think about things – important things:

Leader 2: Like what really matters, and what really doesn't.

Leader 1: Like who should come first in the queue.

Leader 2: Like what we need to hold on to with our hands and our hearts – and what we need to let go.

Leader 1: These are important things, and they deserve out undivided attention.

Leader 2: So take time out of your busy schedule to sit at the feet of Jesus and think about the important things.

Leader 1: Take time to ponder with God ...

Some words for Shrove Tuesday

Everybody, take a minute and look at your feet, and imagine: *Where do your feet take you?* On long walks or a run – down paths and up hills, across bridges, into the fresh air or the biting rain …

Children, close your eyes and imagine: Where do your feet take you? To school, out to play with your friends, to your room to do your homework. They let you play football and dance.

Grown-ups, close your eyes and imagine: Where do your feet take you? To work, down to the Underground or across a train platform or into an office or out on a farm.

Your feet have taken you on so many journeys, but the most important place they can take you is to each other.

Putting down and picking up

An all-age experience

At the front, set a large beautifully wrapped gift.

Reading: Matthew 7:7–12

Leader:

Look at the box – and imagine ......

Children, imagine what might be inside – and imagine it's for you. What is it? It's the one thing you've always wanted, and it can be anything. What is it?

(Take time and let the children answer.)

Grown-ups, look at the box – and imagine. Imagine it is the one gift you can give your children, or your grandchildren, or the children you have come to love. What is it? It's the one thing you can give them, and it can be anything. What is it?

(Take time and let the adults answer.)

Everybody, look at the box – and imagine. Imagine that it is the one gift you can give the world – the people you've never met, who are really so much like us: brothers and sisters we have never seen. What is it? It's the one thing you can give them, and it can be anything. What is it?

(Take time and let folk answer.)

Leader:

My, what a lot of wonderful precious gifts! We thank God for them and ask God to teach us to use them wisely and gratefully.

Isn't it funny, too, that many of the presents we would want to give aren't things really, but priceless gifts: peace, health, education, love …

As we enter into Lent – a time when we consider who we are and who God calls us to be – we lay aside some of the 'things' so we can pick up the gifts.

Prayer:

God who loves us,
teach us to give and to share,
to realise that what we need and what we want
aren't the same thing.
Teach us to care as much for the people we don't see
as the ones we do.

Song: 'Know that God is good' (CH4 788)

Activity/action for a small group:

Have one table laden with things (chocolate, alcohol, watches; think outside the box as every community is unique). Invite people to choose something they'd like to give up during Lent, to pick up one thing and return with it to their seat.

Have another table full of gifts to search for during Lent (Love, Peace, Patience, Balance, Calm; think outside the box as every community is unique). Have these words written on cards, or symbols of these gifts (a heart, a peace sign, a kite …) After some quiet reflective time, or a song (e.g. 'Take this moment', by John Bell, from One Is the Body, *Wild Goose Publications), have folk come forward and put down the thing they chose earlier, and pick up a gift from this table.*

Prayer:

God of the gifts we cannot buy,
only discover,
lead us into Lent.
May our wandering minds find focus and
our restless hearts be still.
May we fill the yearning in our souls
with gifts that satisfy
not stuff that fades away.

And when we return on Easter Day,
may the gifts we have embraced help us
embrace each other.
Amen

Shrove Tuesday pause before the journey

Life is a journey.
We're always heading out to new things –
new experiences, new people to meet, new lessons to learn …
Today, we gather to think about what kind of people we want to be,
what kind of people God calls us to be:
what are the lessons we need to learn
to be ready to walk the way God asks us to go?
The way of love, forgiveness, fairness, kindness, friendship …

I want you to stand really straight and still.
Close your eyes and feel the ground, solid beneath your feet.
Think about all the places your feet take you:
to school, to play with friends, to visit your gran and grandpa …
to work, to the shops, to visit your neighbours –
then off to bed at night and up in the morning –
back on your feet.

Today, we come here to think about
where we want to go in our lives –
but even more important than that:
how we want to get there.
What do we want to leave behind on the road
as a sign of our lives?
Do you want to leave love, kindness, patience, laughter?
Do you want to leave a fairer, more just and equal world?

Leave gentle footprints in your wake,
not scars where you've trampled.

On this day,
at the start of Lent,
decide how you'll walk the way …

Let's have a prayer:

We've gathered with our friends
to think about where our lives need to go.
With feet firmly on the ground,
with hands outstretched to embrace each other,
with minds and spirits open
(with stomachs full of pancakes!)
we are ready to journey –
lead us, Lord.

Ash Wednesday

An Ash Wednesday reflection

Leader's note: Begin by sharing with the congregation a time when you were lost: a story from childhood, or a more recent one, like maybe when your car's satnav sent you the long way round!

Leader:

Lost is a lonely place to be. Forgotten is frightening … Think about a time when you were lost … Turn now and tell your neighbour about it …

Give the congregation time for discussion. Depending on the size of the group, you may want to share some of the stories. At the end of the sharing, call everyone together by singing 'Jesus loves me'.

All sing 'Jesus loves me' …

Finish your story, telling folk about how you were found. Or tell a different story about a time when you were lost and found.

Leader:

When you're found, your whole self says: 'Phew!' When somebody remembers you, it's like … what's it like? … Turn to your neighbour and tell them how it felt to be found and remembered …

Depending on the size of the group, you may want to share some of the stories. At the end of the sharing, call everyone together by singing 'Jesus loves me'.

All sing 'Jesus loves me' …

Leader:

Today is Ash Wednesday: a day when we think about being lost and found. During Lent, we take time to think about who we are, about the good things, and the not so good. God loves us and always holds us, but sometimes we lose ourselves. Lent lets us find ourselves and come back to God.

All sing 'Jesus loves me' ...

Fondant Santas and chocolate bunnies

My, how time flies! It seems like just yesterday that the garden centre was filled with festive cheer – 10-foot blow-up Santas and fibre-optic reindeer. You couldn't go anywhere without hearing Cliff Richard singing 'Mistletoe and wine' or Slade screaming 'It's Christmas...!' I have to admit I was a bit bemused by the chocolate Advent calendars in October, but now they've been replaced with creme eggs and chocolate bunnies in January, so I guess the corporate/consumer launch of Easter is upon us.

Now I don't mean to sound like a Scrooge (it's almost Lent – we mustn't bring Scrooge into it!). I have nothing against chocolate – I'm rather a big fan of the stuff, and I love a celebration as much as the next person. But I *do* worry that there is an important opportunity being missed here – for hidden under all these chocolate bunnies and creme eggs is the ancient call to reflection, and the church needs to reclaim it because the world needs it. Lent is a time to rethink, to reconsider, to reflect on where we're going. Lent is a time, before the celebration of Easter, to consider where some of the paths we follow ultimately lead. If we head in the direction that money, power, success, self-interest leads us … where will we end up?

If we climb the ladder of success in such a way as to ignore the ones around us, where will we find ourselves? Lent is a time to reconsider.

I was asked recently if I thought that, in a 'post-religious' society, church had anything to offer. We have this: We have the clarion call to repentance – not the 'sackcloth and ashes, I am a loathsome sinner' misunderstanding of repentance, but the 'turn around, reconsider, redirect yourselves call to a new way of living'.

Every faith tradition that has stood the test of time has had, at its centre, a sense of the importance of others. When religion becomes a consumer culture primarily focused on personal salvation and 'right' doctrine – when a believer's scales tip towards his/her own individual afterlife rather than living this life in a way that helps to ensure that everyone has as full a life as they can – one has to wonder if they've inadvertently opted for the fondant Santas and chocolate bunnies.

Lent: an opportunity to journey with Jesus and wrestle with yourself. Lent: a time to reconsider, reflect, redirect your life. Lent: an ancient clarion call to change.

My, how time flies! Before you know it, it will be Easter Day. How will you travel there this year?

Meditation for Ash Wednesday

Tonight we stand at the doorway to the desert. Ready to open it into Lent and to walk with Jesus. Here, at the start of Lent, we remember Jesus' baptism in the River Jordan and God's words to him: *'You are my beloved son – with you I am well-pleased.'* Words that, far from warming him into complacency and sending him back home, closed one door firmly behind him – and opened another that led him into the desert, where he questioned who he was, why he was here, and what his life was for; words that sent Jesus into the desert to wrestle with what it meant to be him.

And tonight we, too, are called to walk through a door and into the desert to wrestle with what it means to be us – what it means to walk with Jesus.

Here are some questions that might help. Take a little time to reflect:

- *What would unlock the door and let you do that? ...*
- *What baggage do you need to put down first? ...*
- *What burdens do you need to lay aside? ...*
- *When you come up out of the waters, what words will send you into the desert? ...*

Yesterday the children gathered for Shrove Tuesday – they ate pancakes and ran a bit riot together round the hall and had fun – just because they were together. And there's a lot to be said for that alone. But there was another reason for their gathering: to open the door to reflection for them – to enable them to think about what was important to them, what kind of person they wanted to be ... what kind of person they wanted to become. They decorated their shoes for the journey into Lent, praying to walk a path that leads to love, patience, joy, forgiveness, fairness ... Theology for five-year-olds.

This is the reason for our gathering – because Jesus wants to change our direction: he wants us to close the door on some of the things we thought were really important – and to open our hearts to other people. He wants you to follow him into the desert to reconsider your priorities, revise your presumptions, overturn your prejudices, and revisit painful places where healing may still be needed and your avoidance of them causes festering.

Tonight, Jesus calls you to join him in the story of his baptism – to come up out of the waters with the words: *'You are my beloved – with you I am well-pleased'* ringing in your ears. Refreshed and made clean from the waters, open the door and enter the desert. Marked as sons and daughters of dust and the earth, walk the way of Lent with God and Jesus.

Song/chant: 'Come back to God', by Emily Walker (from *Eggs and Ashes*, Ruth Burgess and Chris Polhill, Wild Goose Publications)

Stations for reflection:

Play some quiet music during the stations. Allow plenty of time: folk can visit one or two or all of the stations.

Station 1: A reminder of your baptism

Location: at the font or place of baptism in the church/building

The leader invites folk to come forward to kneel or stand, and to be sprinkled with water. During this, the leader says: 'You are beloved of God, who says: "With you I am well-pleased." Baptism welcomes you home and sends you out. Go and journey with God.'

Station 2: The shoes

Location: at the back of the font

Leader:

At the back of the font are shoes, ready and waiting for your journey. These were decorated by the children, and represent where we want to find ourselves journeying towards this Lent ... Do we want to journey towards a more loving path, a more forgiving, juster, kinder way? Take time; look at what they've done. Also, there are some extra shoes and pens. If you'd like, write a word, a sign, a name – whatever you want – on the shoes, as an indication of where you hope to travel towards this Lent.

Station 3: The ashes

Location: near the communion table

The leader invites folk to come forward to be marked with ash (with the sign of the cross on their palm or forehead). During this, the leader says: 'From dust you have come, and to dust you shall return' ...

The singing of 'Come back to God' signals folk to return to their seats.

Symbols and searching

The congregation can move in groups to the various locations or, if the group is small, travel together. (This piece can also be used on the first Sunday in Lent.)

Words at the font:

Giving birth to new ideas, nurturing dreams,
encouraging the first fledgling flight into something yet unknown,
and walking beside the tentative footsteps of an early journey.

God, we are baptised into life –
risk-taking, once-only, not-to-be-missed life!
God, we are baptised into life,
for embracing and uplifting and planting seeds
that will spring up long after we're gone.

We dedicate ourselves to you, God,
and will work with this family to bring baptism and life
through its programmes and people.

Response:

Folk are invited to be sprinkled with water, as a reminder of their baptism.

Words at the door:

We stand at the door and knock.
And we can't help but ask:
what's on the other side?

God of the journey, we take steps in faith:
faith that your words will guide us,
your Spirit will challenge us,
your presence will comfort us.
But we won't know what's on the other side
until we open the door
and take the first step.

We dedicate our feet to you.
May they walk the path you dream for us.

They stand at the door and knock:
visitors, friends, strangers who happen upon this house.
We dedicate ourselves to them as well:
when they knock on our door,
we will open it in welcome,
offering kindness, a cup of refreshing water
and a place to lay their heads and hearts in safety.

Response:

Folk are invited to have their palms anointed with oil, as a symbol of giving and receiving hospitality.

Words at the communion table:

You have gathered the world around your table, Christ.
There are no barriers, no barricades, no 'Do not enter' signs
barring the way.
We will follow your rules of hospitality:
whoever sits at our table will be respected

and welcomed and cared for.
All are equally fed at your table, Christ of all.

Response:

Folk are invited to take sweeties from a bowl on the communion table and to share them with others.

Words at the cross:

Never-changing, ever-changing:
the paradox you smile down upon us,
the message of the cross.
You will always love us –
that will never change;
but because you love us,
we are always called to change –
to find new ways to express the eternal message
of your constant affection.

We dedicate ourselves to this mission:
to seek light and new paths,
to ever-change in your never-changing love.

Response:

Folk are invited to lay their hand on the cross.

Ecumenical Ash Wednesday school address

Readings: Joel 2:12–13, 15–17; Matthew 6:16–18

Well, here we are: back together again because Lent has started … Every year since I've been here, I've sat at lunch tables and listened as we've lamented the fact that we gather this way so rarely. And every year, we vow not to let it happen again, but we do. It is a painful admission of our fractured faith in each other; and especially now, as I look out at how beautiful you all look when you're together, I sense the *sense* in God's call for unity. How little it matters whether we say 'debts' or 'sins' or 'trespasses', how little it matters to God whether we sprinkle or dunk, whether our parents take vows or we do, whether we are part of the frozen chosen or the holy rollers – how little all that matters compared with what we *share*. Fellow humans, here we are. Beloved Christian brothers and sisters, we're back together again.

'Blow the trumpet in Zion and ____________ (the name of the town/city)*: sanctify a fast; call a solemn assembly; gather the people. Sanctify the congregation; assemble the aged, gather the children, even infants at the breast. Let the bridegroom leave his room and the bride her canopy. Between the vestibule and the altar, let the priests, the ministers of the Lord, weep.'*

Back together again because Lent has started – the time of heart-rending. Let's not sell that short – because this can be a powerful time for us, if we take it for what it is. God knows we need time in our lives: to grow our spirits, to stretch our resistant souls. Heart-rending can be life-altering.

Yesterday, Shrove Tuesday – that's a funny old day. It began as a day when we are called to cleanse – to empty ourselves in preparation. To sincerely, and painfully sometimes, ask forgiveness so that we can enter the wilderness travelling light – put those cumbersome bags down: lay down guilt, remorse, anger ... Put down, and do not pick up again, bitterness, hate ... lay it down so we can use all our being to wander alone in our wilderness places and make way for the Good News. And what do we do – we have pancake suppers and we spring clean our houses and we give up things for Lent – all in a valiant effort to distract ourselves from the soul-searching, heart-rending call of this sacred sojourn.

Today's New Testament reading is a lesson from Jesus to us as we begin this journey. And when we read these lessons, we must remember that this is someone who loves us more than we can imagine being loved. This is not a fearful warning about an angry God; this is saying: you have an opportunity here to grow your spirits – to stretch your resistant souls. Do not waste it by focusing all that effort in the wrong direction. Do not waste it by rending your clothes but not your hearts; sprucing up the outside, but not digging deep.

A reward is what you'll get in exchange for your effort – if your effort is aimed at getting praise from people, you'll get that ... but you will be storing your treasure up on earth, not in heaven. But if you rend your heart before God alone – if you go to those places in your wilderness and wrestle there, you will grow your spirit. And that is a treasure stored in a place where nothing and no one can steal it away.

'Return to me with all your hearts,' says the Lord. 'With fasting and with weeping and with mourning; rend your hearts and not your clothing. Return to the Lord your God, for God is gracious and merciful, slow to anger and abounding in steadfast love.'

Fellow humans, here we are. Beloved Christian brothers and sisters, we're back together again. As you come forward and receive the ashes on your forehead, place that sign in your heart, and do not waste this sacred time. Go into the wilderness and look for treasure.

Written for churches who gathered in Seneca, South Carolina during Lent

Reflection and all-age Lenten walk

Bible reading: Mark 1:9–13

Leader:

With this, we begin our journey into Lent: a time to think, as Jesus did, about who we are, how we got here, where we're going, and how we're going to get there. A time to reflect and get ourselves right.

We're all at different points in the road, and probably have different needs for the journey. Do you need nourishment … refreshment … direction and guidance? Some time to reflect before taking action? Or a destination: something to aim for? Or protection: something for the hard weather and dangerous places? …

Because today is all about a journey, we are not going to remain in one place, but are going on a 'treasure hunt' around town. At different spots, we'll stop and pick up something to help us on our journey through Lent.

Ideas for the Lenten walk:

Expand on these – be creative:

1. Stop at a bakery and buy a loaf of bread. We all need nourishment to grow and think and become … Share the bread, and think about all those who don't have enough to eat. Talk about what you can do to help them …

2. Stop at a water fountain in a park – take a good long drink. Or go for tea and coffee at a local coffeeshop. Everyone needs water to live, to grow – and to get clean and feel refreshed. Jesus was called 'the living water', and his cleansing, refreshing love helps us to live and grow …

Talk about those in the world who do not have access to clean water. What can you do to help? ...

3. Stop at the Tourist Information Centre or by a road sign. Sometimes we lose our way and need direction – we have family, friends, teachers, ministers; we have all the stories about love in the Bible ... Take a moment to decide on where you want to go next; and on which route you'll take to get back home ...

4. Stop at a bench or a resting place. Talk about the need for space to think, to pray, to reflect on the journey ... Sit together in the quiet for a moment and listen to the sounds of the town/country ...

Dust and ashes and the muddy muddy water

An Ash Wednesday liturgy

Introduction

Bible reading: Joel 2:12–17

Ash Wednesday … the day of repentance that begins the Lenten journey. I've never thought that guilt was a good catalyst for change – it is a dragging, exhausting, crippling thing. Unless it moves you on to somewhere else, it remains a dark barren corner.

Funny, but every year in Lent, we start near the beginning of the end: revisiting the day when Jesus rode into Jerusalem as the talk of the town. Folk waved their palm branches that day – they sang their alleluias and called him their King; but then, the tide turned, and we all know where that triumphal entry ended.

And so today, we return and consider ourselves … The ashes for today's service are traditionally made from the charred remains of last year's palm crosses. These were worn on lapels and waved by excited children and held on to through hosannas: they represent the hope we sing every year, as we remember that first Palm Sunday. Today the ashes are mixed with a little oil, and then placed on foreheads and the palms of hands so that we remember. The ashes represent the charred remains of our good intentions. They are a prayer that this year, this time, there will be a change in us, that we will follow him a little further down the road he walks.

We start near the beginning of the end, and remember and rethink …

There are many theories about where the tradition of the ashes began. Some say it represents our mortality and harks back to the very first story of creation, when God blew into the dust, and out we came: 'From dust you have come, and to dust you will return' (Genesis 3:19).

Some say it is a symbol of mourning and has its origin in times long ago when the cooking fire was in the living quarters, and the hearth needed constant tending so that the ashes didn't cover everything in the house. When there was sorrow at the centre of a household and folk were preoccupied with that overwhelming event, the tragedy would be obvious in people's ashen appearance. Gradually, people intentionally wore the ashes as a sign of sorrow.

No one really knows where the tradition began, but the symbolism permeates tonight's gathering.

We return to the beginning of the end – to acknowledge our mortality.

We return to the beginning of the end – to remember the fragility of our intentions and to pray for strength.

We return to the beginning of the end, entering a time when our day-to-day focus has shifted onto something so much more enduring. We enter a sacred season, and turn towards what is most important: our day-to-day examined in the light of eternity.

Walk into the dust of the desert, and begin again …

Quiet music

Bible reading: John 8:2–11

Meditation:

He bent down, and he drew in the dust of the earth. What did he write? We will never know. Was it about her – her sin, her guilt? … Maybe it was about her partner: like Adam in the very first story, hiding behind the woman? …

Was it about them – the ones holding the stones – about their judgement and harshness? … We will never know because, just like her adultery and their judgement, he did not record it in his heart, but forgave it – forgotten, just like the words traced in the sand.

Tonight is about forgiveness like that: forgiven, forgotten – clean-slate redemption. Tonight is about love like that – a love that doesn't let us get away with wrong but calls us to face it: things we have done, messes we have made, the pointing fingers we try to distract ourselves with, the pointing fingers we use to throw people off our trail …

Tonight is a time to stand in front of God with no disguise or mask or barrier, or fear, and to hear the words you long for:

'I do not condemn you. You are forgiven. Go your way, and from now on do not sin again.'

Tonight, come back to God and whisper your secrets to the Holy Spirit hovering here …

A time of silence

Bible reading: Mark 1:9–12

Meditation:

A picture: shiny white robe, glistening wet hair tossed back against his shoulders: Jesus coming up out of the Jordan with the clear, clean water streaming down his body. The white dove hovering above the whole scene, dimmed only by the aura surrounding Jesus. And that glint of determination in Jesus' eyes as he looks towards the shore and the hot sands of the desert … Pretty cool, huh? Charlton Heston would be proud. My Sunday-school teacher would be amazed that I still remember that picture framed in our classroom: the blond, blue-eyed Jesus in the shiny white robe … It's a good image. (We like that image.) It fits snugly in beside the white lace Christening shawls and the tepid water of the font and the peaceful, cosy, intimate gathering that welcomes an infant.

Another picture: Jesus, no glistening robe to be seen, stripping off his cloak and trudging into the muddy waters of the Jordan, picking his way around the rocks underfoot to get in deep enough. Jesus, holding his breath and being plunged under – coming up, not pure and pretty, but dirty – swamped in the mud of existence: he did not come out clean, but covered in the earth he would walk on, and breathe in and love.

Jesus was baptised into the world, not out of it. The Jordan is and was a muddy hole of a place, so our Sunday-school picture doesn't wash. But we have a far more powerful image – a deeply symbolic call for our lives: baptised in the mud of the earth, turfed out into the thick of it – with these words always echoing: 'With you I am well-pleased.' It's a good image. (We like that image.) It sets the scene for a life of love and forgiveness and real hard work; inspiring and engaging and relevant to our day-to-day. It fits in more with hospital gowns and smelly clothes, the cold cup of water given to a stranger. Dust and ashes and the muddy muddy water …

Time of reflection:

There are three stations for reflection. Folk can go to one, two or all three of the stations; allow plenty of time for this. Include meditative background music.

1: The ashes

Location: at the top of the choir on either side of the communion table

Action: administration of the ashes

Instructions for leader and celebrant: The leader holds the bowl of ashes for the celebrant and recipient. After the recipient comes forward, the celebrant says to them: 'From dust you have come, and to dust you shall return', *then makes the sign of the cross on their palm.*

2: Confession

Location: at the crossing

Action: confession in the sand

Instructions for leader: Each participant is invited to come forward to an area of sand surrounded by stones, and to write a confession in the sand: a word, a name, a picture … After they have finished, the leader says to each person:

Jesus said: 'Has no one condemned you? Neither do I condemn you: Go your way, and from now on do not sin again.'

3: Water

Location: at the font

Action: sending out

Instructions for leader: The leader invites each participant to kneel or stand in front of the font. After each person comes forward, the leader says to them: Called out of the waters of your baptism and into the desert: 'Go, search for God and you'll find yourself too', *then sprinkles them with water.*

'Return to God', by Marty Haugen (GIA Publications), is the signal for folk to begin to take their seats.

Song: 'Return to God'

On taking action

Come in

God says: 'Come in,
sit down, pull up a chair –
you're welcome here.'

God says: 'Come in,
roll up your sleeves, there's work to do –
you're needed here.'

God says: 'Come in and go out,
rest and work, live and love
and learn in my company –
you're mine and I love you.'

God says: 'Come in.'

There's lots of work to do

New kid on the block or in with the bricks, fresh face or old hand, you are welcome here, and you are needed too. People of God, here's what we have to do.

MOVE OVER, MAKE ROOM – THERE'S LOTS OF WORK TO DO!

Early-riser or sleepyhead, first out of the starting blocks or comeback kid, adrenaline junkie or quiet thinker, you are welcome here, and you are needed too. People of God, here's what we have to do.

MOVE OVER, MAKE ROOM – THERE'S LOTS OF WORK TO DO!

Our generous God has a big to-do list for the church and that's not going to happen by itself. The church is the body that will live out God's big plans and everybody is welcome and needed. So, people of God, you know what you have to do.

MOVE OVER, MAKE ROOM – THERE'S LOTS OF WORK TO DO!

Here and there God

Here and there God –
you who spin the planets and set the stars alight
and sit at our tables and share our stories,
we come calling on you,
because alone we cannot wipe it away –
not even with our tears, God –
the injustice, the pain, the humiliation
that takes up residence in some places.
We can't just rinse it down and dry it off;
smooth some balm over it and hope it heals,
much as we're desperate to.

Overwhelmed with it all,
we sometimes hide in the corner of our comfortable lives,
sending platitudes from a safe distance, like a Hallmark card.

At other tables,
people go hungry.
At other tables,
some sit abused and frightened
and forgotten.

At other tables,
our neighbours live with war in residence next door.
Help us to turn the tables and dry tears
and come out of our comfortable corners.
We here ask that you send us there.
Amen

Bloom where you're planted

God, you call us to bloom where we're planted,
to open ourselves to your potential
wherever we find ourselves.

Forgive us when we refuse to open anything –
much less our hands or hearts or minds.
Forgive us when we plant only our will in your way.

When we find ourselves afraid of your Spirit,
forgive us and find us where we hide.
Call us out of the shadows
and plant us where you will.
Grow us, God.
Amen

Body talk

Voice 1: Good morning. We've been sent specially to talk to you, because we are experts in working together.

Voice 2: Oh yes! We are part of a wonderful thing – a thing made of lots of other things.

Voice 1: And without every single little thing,

Voice 2: The one thing wouldn't work the wonderful way it does.

Voice 1: Believe it or not, we are both different parts of the same body!

Voice 2: Betcha can't guess which parts we are.

Voice 1: We're both important.

Voice 2: Really important!

Voice 1: Go on, guess! *(Let the children guess.)*

Voice 2: You're very clever – all those parts are really important.

Voice 1: We wouldn't know what to do without them.

Voice 2: But that's not who we are.

Voice 1: No, you haven't guessed.

Voice 2: My important friend here is the epiglottis. Anybody know what that is? *(Let the children answer.)*

She stays at the back of the throat and protects the windpipe. That's the tube that takes the air down into your lungs. Problem is, another tube that takes the food to the stomach stays just next door, so if you eat too fast, the food sometimes goes down the wrong way. The epiglottis is a flap that flops down over the windpipe and stops the food going there and choking you. Pretty clever, huh?! So, without her, the body would be in big trouble.

Voice 1: Thank you. You're too kind. But if you think *I'm* important – my friend here is *amazing*! She lives just inside the ear. She's called the ear canal and she is in charge of making some pretty important stuff. Earwax! That's that gunky stuff that protects the canal. Earwax has chemicals in it that fight off infections that could hurt the rest of the ear and make it hard to hear. It also collects dirt to help keep the ear canal clean. So earwax isn't just gross. It's gross and useful.

Voice 2: *(Looking/sounding a bit embarrassed)* So you see, we're all important. The one wonderful body wouldn't work the wonderful way it does if we weren't there.

Voice 1: So, our advice to you somebodies is to be more like us.

Voice 2: Yeah: find your place and do your job the best you can.

Voice 1: You, the church – yep, that's you! – are called the Body of Christ.

Voice 2: Because you are all important parts of one big, wonderful thing.

Voice 1: Without you, the Body of Christ, the one big thing on earth that helps Jesus get good things done …

Voice 2: Just wouldn't be complete.

Voice 1: You all have a special part to play to make the church work.

Voice 2: So, somebodies – get to it. Find your part and then do it the best you can.

Voice 1: Over the next couple of weeks, other members of the body are going to come and introduce themselves.

Voice 2: Other parts of the church body, that is. And they'll tell you where they work.

All the little things you do

Every epic journey begins with a step: one at a time, we take ourselves to a new place. Our 'becoming' doesn't happen all at once, but is a gradual evolution and a turning. During this time of Lenten reflection, take some small steps – see where they lead you.

Here are some ideas to start you off …

1. Throw a stone into still water. Watch the ripples it makes. When you do something kind, love ripples out to others. Do something kind today for someone.

2. Consider making this Lenten promise: For forty days, when you're buying something, ask yourself the question: Is this something I *need*? Then act accordingly.

3. Silence is a rare gift. Find time (every day, once a week: whatever you can create for yourself) to sit in silence and listen for God.

4. Everybody needs to try different things – it keeps life interesting! Take a

taste of something you've never tried before, or go somewhere you've never been.

5. Set an extra place at the table each day. Think about who might join you ... remember people in the world who are hungry and who would love to sit down and share a meal.

Walk his way

An all-age activity for Lent

This is a super way to get all ages to share in an activity, and can be done on Shrove Tuesday or Ash Wednesday; alternatively, before or after church on the first Sunday of Lent (whichever works in your situation). You can also make this a Sunday-school activity.

You will need sidewalk chalk and a sizable area of pavement.

Write: 'Jesus says: Follow me' and draw two footprints beside the words.

Have the participants trace their own footprints along a path and write their name. Older ones can add a word, phrase or sentence expressing what following might mean to them: e.g. 'adventure', 'risk', 'friendship', 'sharing' ...

Lead us not into temptation

As this day begins,
as the world spins in its perpetual orbit
and things happen as they will,
God of us all,
lead us not into the temptation
of deciding that we have nothing to do with it.
Easy as it might be to sit back
and just let things spin on,
help us to take our lives in hand.
Give us the courage to let go of some of the things
that keep us from being the people
you have created us to be.
Grow our wisdom
so that we learn to distinguish between
the unchangeable random nature of life
and the things that we can impact for good or ill.
Forgive our faltering progress and our wandering.
Turn even that into lessons that heal
and move us forward.
In your mysterious yearning for goodness,
we find your Spirit stirring in places
we thought closed off and barren.
Continue that work, Spirit of all.
Nudge and nurture the possibilities
we have to help your goodness grow.
God of love – live in us.
Amen

Good things from small things

A little yeast makes the dough rise, and it becomes something yummy to eat. Tiny seeds are planted and they become trees that give us shade.

GOOD THINGS COME FROM SMALL THINGS.

Just one kind word makes the lonely times better, a little cuddle makes the sad times easier, a helping hand makes the work less of a burden.

GOOD THINGS COME FROM SMALL THINGS.

A wee idea can become a plan, and a plan can grow into a reality that makes life better for people. A chance meeting can grow into friendship and friendship into a love that lasts a lifetime.

GOOD THINGS COME FROM SMALL THINGS.

All the little kindnesses, all the new ideas, all the meetings and moments and wee bits of magic can grow and grow. You never know until you begin.

GOOD THINGS COME FROM SMALL THINGS
AND GOD IS IN IT ALL.

Go out of your way today to do one small thing to change your small corner of this big, wide world.

On love

Mother God

A liturgy for Mothering Sunday

A calling to mind:

We will begin not with a call to worship, but with a calling to mind …

Call to mind someone you love. Close your eyes and imagine: the shape of her eyes, the curve of his smile, the sound of their laughter …

Call to mind … the way he smells, the way she feels – and the look they give you that says 'I've had enough' …

If you can hold that face, that feeling, that love, then consider this:

One hundred trillion cells, seven million years of evolution, forty weeks of gestation, years of love and lessons and laughter – tears too no doubt – have gone into that person you brought to mind who holds your heart – what a wonder.

Think on it …

And now, think on this:

The planet holds over 7 billion souls – every single one a unique one-off-never-to-be-repeated-ever creation: the creative imagination of the divine is reflected in every face. The Spirit of God is in every first and last and in-between breath.

Mother God, thank you for our family – as vast as the ocean, as intimate as a face, a smell, a touch, a look, a feeling …

(Pause)

'Body of Christ', 'Family of God', 'Brothers and sisters in the Lord': on this Mothering Sunday we remember what these words mean, and we are called never to underestimate the deep desire with which God created this vision: it is so important that the world remembers that no one is an only child.

Song: 'Brother, sister, let me serve you', by Richard A.M. Gillard and Betty Jane Pulkingham (CH4 694)

Reflection: 'Mother's days'

Shekinah,[1] Mother-God … You moved over the waters at the birth of creation: the palpable silence before sound, the midwife of our moments, yet embodying eternity. At the beginning of the beginning, you moved over the face of creation, scanning every feature, drinking in each tiny detail, already besotted. Holy, wholly Spirit, you breathe and become with us.

Mother God, you were there in the burning bush, in the pillar of cloud – and of fire; you hovered close and wrapped yourself around Hagar as she wept in exile with her son. When Israel was a child, you loved him, taught him to walk, took him in your arms, fed him with your body and kindness …

Your cry joined Rachel's in Ramah as she wept for her children – your keen-ing pierced the sky as you refused to be comforted.

Yearning in your depths, you longed to gather your children together, as a hen gathers her chicks under her wings.

Still unable to keep silent, you birth the wonders that come into being – in our hearts, in our hands, all our days, all the days that are.

And when our days are ended, you wrap yourself around us, scoop us up and cradle us home. You will not forget us, cannot forget us, any more than a mother – eternally besotted – can forget the baby at her breast, the child of her heart, the love of her life …

Bath-kol: voice,
Torah: teaching,
Racham: compassion,
Hokhma: wisdom,
Ruach ha-kodesh: Holy Spirit,
come.

Midwife of our every moment,
embodying eternity,
Holy, wholly Spirit …
breathe and become with us.

Song: 'Enemy of Apathy (She sits like a bird)', by John L. Bell and Graham Maule (CH4 593), or in *Iona Abbey Music Book* or *Enemy of Apathy* (Wild Goose Publications)

Prayer:

Before you were born,
my body held you in secret.
As you learned to walk,
I held your hand.
When you let go
and ventured out into your bright new day,
I held my breath.

Bone of my bone …
flesh of my flesh …
beat of my heart …

spark of eternity …
gift to the world …

you were never mine to hold on to forever,
but my heart can't help it.

Child of mine, wherever you go,
my love, my life, my dreams
and the constant whisper of my prayers,
go with you.

Response: ('Bless the Lord', Kenyan traditional song, CH4 756)

Mother, we hear you calling:

'Bone of my bone …
flesh of my flesh …
beat of my heart …
spark of eternity …
gift to the world …
come home.
Come home.'

God our mother,
your voice echoes all around us.
We catch hints of your pleading in the cries of the hungry,
snatches of your pleasure in the laughter of our children,
new verses of your song in every dawn chorus.
Mother of all, we share the breath of your creative spirit
and your imprint is on every soul.
Teach us to see you in each other.
Holy, wholly Spirit,
forgive us when we wander away:

when we forget who we are and why we're here –
when we fragment ourselves and forget that we are family.
Gather us again under your wings and under the roof of your heaven
that we may open the doors of our hearts to each other
and share this planet-home.
Mother, we hear you calling:

'Bone of my bone …
flesh of my flesh …
beat of my heart …
spark of eternity …
gift to the world …
come home.
Come home.'

Amen

Response: ('Bless the Lord')

Song: 'Mothering God', by John L. Bell (CH4 117), or in *Iona Abbey Music Book*, or *I Will Not Sing Alone* (Wild Goose Publications)

Blessing:

Beloved of God – that is exactly who you are –
a unique-one-off-never-to-be-repeated-ever creation …
just like everyone else.
Go in the knowledge of that overwhelming love
and embrace your family.
Amen

Note:

1. Shekinah (also Shechinah, Shechina or Schechinah) is an ancient Jewish concept of God in the feminine. The word originally comes from 'dwelling' or 'settling'. Grammatically and conceptually feminine, the Shekinah denoted the divine settling of God's spirit among the people. Shekinah was associated with the 'burning bush', the pillar of cloud and fire that stayed close and guided the children of Israel, the thick smoke on Sinai (Exodus 24:16–18). She was the angel-presence in the story of Hagar, the spirit of God in the Tabernacle and the Temple, and she is the Divine presence that will follow the exiled people wherever they go or are taken. She is closely associated with 'the glory of God'.

   There are other intensely feminine images for God, which offer us different faces and understandings to explore: Bath-kol, or the voice of God, is translated as 'daughter of a voice'. Torah means teaching or instruction, and can be broadly seen as the teaching and practice of the Jewish faith, or more specifically, the words contained in the Pentateuch. The root is feminine. Racham means 'compassion'. It translates as 'mercy from the womb or bowels'.

   Hokhma means 'wisdom', and is used to refer to a wise student or one with insight. Ruach ha-kodesh, or the 'spirit breath of God', is the spirit that hovered over the waters at the birth of creation in Genesis.

Humans being

They say that to err is human, to forgive, divine … but we can manage it too, if we try. When people annoy us, when they make us mad, when they let us down and stress us out, what is it we need to remember?

FORGIVENESS IS A GIFT AND LOVE CAN GIVE IT.

They say, 'We're only human', but that can be a cop-out. Humans being their best can offer reconciliation rather than revenge. Humans being their best can love and let love. When people annoy us, when they make us mad, when they let us down and stress us out, what is it we need to remember?

FORGIVENESS IS A GIFT AND LOVE CAN GIVE IT.

What would you give your children?

What would you give your children? … Every advantage, a head start in life, the best of everything? Is that really the best? What do they need?

LOVE.

What should you give your children? A safe place to learn to fail, a loving place to learn to share, experiences that gently show them that, although they are the light and love of your life, they are not the centre of the universe: they are part of a big wide world. Because what they'll really need is …

LOVE.

What a gift our children are! What a responsibility. We come knowing that we cannot do this raising of them on our own, but need love that explodes our boundaries. The wisest eyes see a glimmer of God in everyone they meet and treat them accordingly.

GOD, TEACH US THIS WISDOM
AND HELP US TO HAND IT DOWN TO OUR CHILDREN.

AND WHEN WE SEE YOU, GOD,
NATURALLY BUBBLING UP IN THEIR LIVES,
HELP US TO ENCOURAGE YOU.
LET US LEARN AND LIVE WHAT WE NEED –
LOVE.

Love one another

A new command I give you: *'Love one another. As I have loved you, so you must love one another.'* That's what Jesus said – the last time they were together.

His friends couldn't remember it all then, so he made sure he left them with the important one.

What would that look like – when lived out ... stretched out over the centuries ... echoed through generations ... played out in the lives of the ones touched by his spirit?

Sadly, I think we've far too often chosen to change that word 'love' – to put in other more worldly-wise favourites; more conventional, understandable, doable-in-the-world-we-have-to-live-in words. Here are some words I've heard try to take over:

Little children: have *control*, one over another.

History has been plagued with this editing job. Any time religion uses fear of an angry God, any time faith becomes a forced legislated thing rather than a response to grace, love has been removed and control has slipped in.

Little children, *sit in judgement*, one over another.

Oh, how we love to substitute this for love – I mean, after all, somebody has to decide who's right and who's wrong. But when we do that, when we decide we have *'the answer'*, we stop listening to each other. Surely listening is the first step to loving. Jesus never said he was the answer: he said he was the way, and if you got on the road with him, he would walk with you and be a light for your path. He told us stories, threw down challenges, sent the Spirit as one of his last gifts – because we weren't near finished and there was a lot more to learn. Jesus is the bread of life and the source of living water – stuff for the journey.

So, he didn't say control or judge or have all the answers, he didn't say that. He said love.

'Little children, love one another' – and when the decision has to be made, when push comes to shove – when we have to choose whether to remember the important thing – love – or to edit it out and put in another one, a more worldly-wise favourite, a more conventional, understandable, doable-in-the-world-we-have-to-live-in word – we need to be brave enough to listen to him. Love trumped tradition, control, judgement, the answers that had held sway in his life, all his life.

'A new command I give you: Love one another. As I have loved you, so you must love one another.' That's what he said – the last time they were together.

They wouldn't remember everything he said, so he made sure he left them with the important one.

The innkeeper

The Good Samaritan … it struck me as I re-read this story recently that the one who really ought to get the credit isn't the Samaritan … Granted, he braves the return of the thieves and he binds the wounds of a stranger. True, he shows almost unbelievable kindness and concern; but then he hands the innkeeper a couple of quid and leaves the real dirty work to someone else. It is the innkeeper who has to finish the job … It is the innkeeper who will care and toil and nurse day after day after day … It is the innkeeper who will listen to the fear and anger and frustration of this abused and wounded person … It is the innkeeper who takes on the responsibility to keep on caring even when he's had more than enough … and it's the innkeeper who has taken this sometimes thankless job on faith, trusting that the Samaritan is good on his word that he will in some way return. Sound familiar?

On not leave-taking

One of my favourite books is *The Book Thief,* by Markus Zusak, and one of the most beautiful quotes in it is spoken by 'Death', who is the narrator of the novel. Death gives a new definition of love: *'Not leaving … an act of trust and love, often deciphered by children.'*

Love is about 'not leaving' – not leaving those in the world who frighten you, offend you, don't think or speak or look like you. Love is about 'not leaving' – not leaving when there is something you can do to help; not leaving, even when there isn't anything to do but be there.

Love is not leaving.

I dreamed of Aunt Rosie last night

I dreamed of Aunt Rosie last night. It was a dream from childhood. We were in the kitchen of the Sea Pines house: the house of parsley, personal boxes of Pop Tarts, toasted peanut-butter-and-jelly sandwiches with the crusts cut off – heaven for a child.

I sat on the old stool, the one with the orange vinyl top that Aunt Rosie used as a stepladder. I remember you could sit on it like a stool, or you could sit on the very top step with the lid open, then it was a chair. That's the way I was sitting, arms propped up on the counter, listening. The grown-ups were talking safe-feeling grown-up talk – the kind of murmurings that felt good with sunburn. Words floated about in my dream: 'Darling, could you pass me that?' …

I could smell Aunt Rosie's perfume – a fragrance that still has the power to draw me back to the beach or Christmas morning, no matter where I am.

I woke up with an ache of longing, but more than that, a sense of eternity – connectedness to all who lived and loved and learned from Aunt Rosie … so this memory is for all of us who sat on the very top step of an orange vinyl step-stool and felt what love was like. I hope it is something that we are able in some way to translate to the ones who've come after. Love has a way of living on long after the lover has left us.

I dreamed of Aunt Rosie last night. I know it will not be the last time.

God of the ebb and flow

Voice 1 (mother of a young child – really poignant if she is holding a baby):

We are all yours, God of our beginnings … we are tiny and fragile and vulnerable, absorbing your world in our every moment; its future, though we as yet do not know it. We need everything done for us; but what we need most is love … Cradle us as we begin our journey. Tuck us up in your love.

Voice 2 (child):

We are all yours, God of our delight … we are raucous and wild – running round your world and your church like dervishes. We make you smile. We make our parents squirm. We innocently ask the unanswerable, and we take the fumbling responses we get in our stride … Walk beside us in case we fall. Give us freedom so we can learn for ourselves.

Voice 3 (youth):

We are all yours, God of our awkwardness … we are outgrowing ourselves, restless and searching – moody sometimes, but who can blame us … we are no longer children, but not yet adults. We ask the unanswerable, but this time we want answers. Meet us in our searching. Let us talk and rave to you when we are awash with new feelings … Stand near as we find our own way.

Voice 4 (adult):

We are all yours, God of the ebb and flow … and though our bodies have calmed, our hearts still search. Happy and sad, rich and poor, mundane and frantic, life dances and limps on its way. We've been deemed to be adults, though sometimes secretly doubt it. The 'magic' we assumed would quell our fears and instil that 'grown-up' confidence we witnessed as children hasn't seemed to work on us. Walk beside us, God. Sing to our hearts … Remind us that we are always your children. Help us find joy in the ebb and flow that is life.

Voice 5 (older person):

We are all yours, God of our years … and though our bodies have slowed, our hearts and minds still search. Life is a strange mixture of present and past. We see ourselves in our children, and in the lives of those who've shared with us (sometimes a blessing; sometimes a curse). And sometimes looking back is easier than looking ahead. Be with us, God, as much now as you were at the beginning … Speak to our souls; whisper your promises again in our hearts. Inspire us to use what we've learned about your world to help those you love.

All:

God of beginning and ending and beginning again, call your family together. Remind us that your family is as vast as the ocean, as different as each moment, but all one in you. Bring us together … for together is your ultimate prayer. Amen

Also by Sally Foster-Fulton

Hope Was Heard Singing: Resources for Advent

An Advent collection of prayers, meditations, poems and a few wee plays. A rich resource, from an original voice, for personal reflection and for congregations and small groups searching for material relevant to the 21st century.

ISBN: 9781849522786

Step Gently in the World: Resources for Holy Week

Reflections, meditations, prayers and liturgies for Holy Week following the journey of Jesus from Palm Sunday to Easter Day. A book which affirms that, even in the darkness of betrayal and denial and death, we can rise up and live different lives: where the justice, peace and love poured out in Christ's life can be resurrected in our own.

ISBN: 9781849523271

Wild Goose Publications is part of the Iona Community ...

- An ecumenical movement of men and women from different walks of life and different traditions in the Christian church
- Committed to the gospel of Jesus Christ, and to following where that leads, even into the unknown
- Engaged together, and with people of goodwill across the world, in acting, reflecting and praying for justice, peace and the integrity of creation
- Convinced that the inclusive community we seek must be embodied in the community we practise

Together with our staff, we are responsible for:

- Our islands residential centres of Iona Abbey, the MacLeod Centre on Iona, and Camas Adventure Centre on the Ross of Mull

and in Glasgow:

- The administration of the Community
- Our work with young people
- Our publishing house, Wild Goose Publications
- Our association in the revitalising of worship with the Wild Goose Resource Group

The Iona Community was founded in Glasgow in 1938 by George MacLeod, minister, visionary and prophetic witness for peace, in the context of the poverty and despair of the Depression. Its original task of rebuilding the monastic ruins of Iona Abbey became a sign of hopeful rebuilding of community in Scotland and beyond. Today, we are about 250 Members, mostly in Britain, and 1500 Associate Members, with 1400 Friends worldwide. Together and apart, 'we follow the light we have, and pray for more light'.

For information on the Iona Community contact:
The Iona Community, Fourth Floor, Savoy House, 140 Sauchiehall Street, Glasgow G2 3DH, UK. Phone: 0141 332 6343
e-mail: admin@iona.org.uk; web: www.iona.org.uk

For enquiries about visiting Iona, please contact:
Iona Abbey, Isle of Iona, Argyll PA76 6SN, UK. Phone: 01681 700404
e-mail: ionacomm@iona.org.uk

Wild Goose Publications, the publishing house of the Iona Community established in the Celtic Christian tradition of Saint Columba, produces books, e-books, CDs and digital downloads on:

- holistic spirituality
- social justice
- political and peace issues
- healing
- innovative approaches to worship
- song in worship, including the work of the Wild Goose Resource Group
- material for meditation and reflection

For more information:

Wild Goose Publications
Fourth Floor, Savoy House
140 Sauchiehall Street,
Glasgow G2 3DH, UK

Tel. +44 (0)141 332 6292
Fax +44 (0)141 332 1090
e-mail: admin@ionabooks.com

or visit our website at
www.ionabooks.com
for details of all our products and online sales